IN FOR A
pound

IN FOR A
pund

MY JOURNEY FROM A MARKET STALL TO
THREE HUNDRED HIGH STREET STORES

CHRIS EDWARDS

WITH STAFFORD HILDRED

JB

JOHN BLAKE

Published by John Blake Publishing Ltd,
3 Bramber Court, 2 Bramber Road,
London W14 9PB, England

www.johnblakebooks.com

www.facebook.com/johnblakebooks **f**
twitter.com/jblakebooks **t**

This edition published in 2015

ISBN: 978 1 78606 026 6

British Library Cataloguing-in-Publication Data:

A catalogue record for this book is available from the British Library.

Design by www.envydesign.co.uk

Printed in Great Britain by CPI Group (UK) Ltd

1 3 5 7 9 10 8 6 4 2

Papers used by John Blake Publishing are natural, recyclable products made from
wood grown in sustainable forests. The manufacturing processes conform to the
environmental regulations of the country of origin.

Every attempt has been made to contact the relevant copyright-holders, but some
were unobtainable. We would be grateful if the appropriate people could contact us.

CONTENTS

PREFACE

My working life so far has been quite a journey, so I decided to share some of it with anyone who's interested. Somehow it has turned into a book, which is a bit of a surprise to me. I've hardly ever had time to read a book let alone write one!

It's for friends, customers and anyone who is interested. My all-important family already know it all, because they have lived it with me. It's not really an autobiography, full of shocking personal revelations and juicy scandal. That's partly because I've been much too busy working to go far off the straight and narrow and mainly because this is a book about the ups and downs of running your own business.

It's about how determination, hard work and a loving family can take a lad, with not much education but plenty of drive, from a stall on Wakefield market to a high street chain of more than 300 shops, while also establishing nine successful nightclubs.

An overwhelming fear of being skint helps too.

INTRODUCTION

'Del Boy' Trotter earned countless richly deserved laughs with his hilarious journey from market trader to millionaire in my favourite television series, *Only Fools and Horses*. I love the British comedy show, which ran from 1981–2003 on BBC1, because it portrays the family side of the market world that I know so well with such compelling warmth and humanity. Creator John Sullivan's wonderful scripts capture the remarkable way of life of stallholders, who often have little more to live on than their wits. Del and Rodney Trotter, the two brothers at the centre of the action, are so beautifully played by David Jason and Nicholas Lyndhurst that as I relax into an episode, it always feels more like real life than entertainment.

Del is my favourite character possibly because at times he seems to have been living a life that is more than a little like my own. It's been more than fifty years since I set off on what has turned out to be an amazingly similar trip. With my younger brother Laurie as my partner, we have worked for more than half a century to grow from running a stall on Wakefield Market in West Yorkshire to building our business into the retail success story that is Poundworld, with 300 shops and more than 6,000 employees around the UK.

It's a journey I wanted to share with family and friends and so at the beginning of 2015, the year in which I faced my sixty-fifth birthday with absolutely no thoughts of retirement, I started writing this book. At the same time Poundworld went into talks with venture capitalists about a possible sale of a majority share in the business. I tried not to think too much about Del Boy's endlessly repeated mantra, 'This time next year, Rodney, we'll be millionaires,' but the parallel was there for all to see.

The negotiations were long and complex but the outcome was that on 15 May 2015, we sold 75 per cent of the business to the American private equity firm TPG for £150 million. I'm staying on as chief executive and my son Christopher will continue as a senior director. Our hearts are still in the business, but more on that later...

CHAPTER ONE

CHILDHOOD DAYS

My childhood began at Saltburn-by-the-Sea, in North Yorkshire, in 2 June 1950, but I didn't stay there long. In fact, I didn't stay anywhere long. I had the great, good fortune to be born into a warm and loving fairground family and all my early life was lived on the move. With my mum Alice, my dad Chris (a name I inherited in true fairground tradition) and my younger brother Laurie, we travelled the fairs of the north of England.

My first memories are almost all of living on the fairground, I suppose, because I was born into that world. I can remember after Laurie was born on 12 April 1953 I was sitting in the car when we picked up my mum and my little baby brother from the maternity hospital. He was in my mother's arms and I was sitting next to them as we left the hospital together. Laurie and I were always very close. We went to the same

1

schools, but I was almost three years older, which is a massive gap when you're really young. As we grew older it seemed to narrow and although we've had plenty of differences over the years, we've always been the best of friends.

To us travelling from place to place seemed a perfectly normal way to spend your life – you certainly never had time to get bored with your surroundings. But my dad was always looking for ways to improve things financially for us as a family and so he took on market stalls to supplement our income from the fairground. The stall I remember most clearly is the one in Wakefield. It was not far from the Cathedral Primary School I attended when we weren't away travelling. My parents would be working there and I'd come back from school to help them pack up before we could go home.

But the fairground was always the place where I really belonged. Everywhere else I went, I felt like I was stepping out to do a job. The fairground was my home. It seemed safe and friendly; it was also a very confined environment where there were no outsiders. Almost everyone was related and it was a great section of society to grow up in. Not everyone realises that the fairground world is very ordered and carefully controlled by the Showmen's Guild of Great Britain, which was founded way back in 1889. The travelling fairs of this country have a long history dating back to Royal Charters, which were granted hundreds of years ago. Anyone who thinks that fairground folk are little more than unruly bunches of trouble-makers is very wide of the mark; they are not like that at all. Every fair is organised by the Showmen's Guild and if you're not a Guild member, you can't go to those fairs. Well run, tightly-knit and not all that welcoming to outsiders, the

Guild is a very English organisation that you have to be born into. Even now, it is pretty much a closed shop. Most people don't realise there is a real code between showmen and a great tradition upheld to this day. I will always be very proud that my family is part of that history.

Traditionally, most marriages were within the fairground world and anyone who married someone outside that special environment would find him or herself frowned upon by their peers, as I would later discover for myself. In those days, 'mixed marriages' as they were known were certainly not popular, although they have always happened. My maternal grandfather was seen as an outsider when he married my grandma. He was an electrician and wasn't fairground oriented at all, but gradually he became accepted – although it took a long time, I've been told.

I haven't really been in the fairground business since I was twenty-one or twenty-two, yet I still feel I belong. Once you are born into a fairground family, and into the wider general fairground family, you are always treated as though you belong. Everybody treats you exactly the same because it is in your blood. The national paper for showmen is called the *World's Fair* and I still read it to this day. There are so many familiar names in the magazine because children are often named after their parents. I read about babies who are given the names of people I knew fifty years ago. Showmen are a very proud and patriotic group of people. On Remembrance Day at the Cenotaph on London's Whitehall, every November, there is always a big group from the fairground world.

As a kid I always felt the best thing about living on the travelling fairground was that it kept me away from school so much. From Easter to October I hardly ever went to school and for a pretty non-academic kid like me that was a plus, obviously. Sometimes I would be squeezed in to some school or other for a few lessons but every week or fortnight we would be travelling so it hardly ever happened. I was happy to stay away. Occasionally someone from the Local Authority would come and say, 'Why isn't he at school?' but by that time we would be heading off somewhere new. It was wonderful! The only time I remember being forced to attend school for two weeks was in a village called North Ormesby, outside Middlesbrough. I felt like an alien – everyone seemed to be looking at me and asking each other: 'Who's he?' It was awful. I only ever went there the one time.

In the fairground world it is all about work, not education. 'If you don't work, you don't get' was the order of my day. From a very early age you are taught: 'You've got to work to earn your money, there's no free meal ticket here'. I think that is where I got my strong work ethic. I had to work at the fairground or behind a stall from when I was very young, maybe seven or eight years old, but I never minded the work – it was just the way it was. Most kids my age would go home to a house. I went home to what they used to call a wagon or a trailer, depending on which kind we had at the time. The old-fashioned one was called a wagon and the new ones were known as trailers.

For years I lived in a wagon as a child. At the time it seemed big, but of course nowadays when I go and visit friends in that world the wagons don't seem so big. Totally modernised, they have gone along with the times. They are fantastic living quarters now, way beyond anything you could have imagined in my day. In our wagon there were three rooms: a kitchen, living room and a bedroom. When my brother and me got a little bit bigger we had what you'd today call a small touring caravan (we called it a trailer). Laurie and I moved in there and for years it was our home. It sounds quite idyllic, travelling the country and not going to school, and in many ways it was. Every year there is a set sequence of fairs. Everyone had their own choice of fairs and chose different places to go. In the early days we used to go to Darlington for Easter, although that eventually changed and we started going to York for Easter instead because the momentum of the fairs was changing and we decided York was a better option. The whole annual calendar of fairs was set out well in advance and occasionally we'd get a gap, or sometimes we would go somewhere different. In my day we found the people from fairgrounds in Lancashire more or less stayed over there all the time whereas showmen from the northeast stayed more or less in that area, and Yorkshire folk generally stayed in that county. We used to mainly cover Lancashire, Yorkshire and the northeast. If you ever went down as far as London, it was completely out of the ordinary and tended to be a one-off. The sort of equipment we could afford was limited. I'm not saying it was primitive and dated but I doubt very much whether we could have got to London! Now all that has changed. Friends who have over the years massively developed their fairground businesses are much more enterprising – today, they go to Dubai or Hong Kong, etc, etc.

When I was a boy my mum and dad's fairground business was fairly modest. We didn't own any of the big flashy rides; all we had were fairground stalls, rifle ranges and coconut shies. They brought us a living, but it was fairly small-scale stuff and quite a comedown compared to what the family business had once been. Many years and a few generations earlier my great-grandfather, Chris Johnson, had been very well known as the head of one of the richer family fairground firms. Some of my ancestors were even famous tightrope walkers, sometimes clowns and all sorts –'sometimes clowns' being the operative words! But every family has its characters and its ups and downs when it comes to wealth. I believe my dad's grandad, my great-grandad, was in his prime in the early 1900s. One of the top operators, with a valuable collection of some of the best fairground rides, he had several children but instead of sharing his wealth out among them in his will, he left most of his estate to just one of his sons, who was apparently the apple of his eye. My dad's mother, my grandma, along with the other brothers and sisters got nothing at all. Worse still, the fortunate brother who inherited everything decided to take the money and run. He sold all the large and lucrative rides, bought himself a big house in Harrogate and left the fairground world altogether.

It was to prove devastating for his brothers and sisters. Destitute might be too strong a word because no one starved, but they were left very hard up and struggling. My dad's mother was one of those siblings who missed out on the wealth. She suffered some very tough times, but she was a wonderful lady and in her later life she and I became very close. When I was growing up I would often find myself working with her on my stall. One of my most prized possessions is a photograph of my grandma helping on my stall in Wakefield. It is hung up in our boardroom, where it serves as a daily reminder to me of where I started. My amazing grandma helped me so much over many years.

I never met my grandad because he died long before I was born. My dad was only eleven years old when his father passed away, so my grandma was left with a very tough situation. The eldest child in the family, Dad had a brother called William who was ten years younger than him and a sister, Brenda, who was seven years younger than my dad, so he had to be a man before he became a boy – at least that's what my mother and grandmother told me. So my grandmother was born into a highly prosperous travelling family, whose wealth then plummeted to zero as the money suddenly went out of the family and they were forced back to basics.

My grandmother and my dad were reduced to trying to earn a living from small enterprises, mainly buying and selling various goods. Then my dad got married and as well as my mum, he had to look after his mother and younger siblings at the same time, so he started from a pretty low baseline.

Mum recalls she had a very difficult start to her married life but she is a great example of what you can achieve with hard work. She was an inspiration to me when I was growing up, and she still is today. Naturally, being my mum, she knows so much more about the early days of our family than me so I'll let her take over for a while.

Alice Edwards says: 'We certainly come from a colourful family background. There was great-great-great-Aunt Louisa, who was a famed tightrope walker and once walked the tightrope strung right across Whitby Harbour, I was told. It was a remarkable feat. She did it for the money raised in collections from the crowds, and the family story goes that when she first tried it, not that many people were gathered, so she deliberately fell off! Louisa vowed to try again the next day and this time the crowds were much larger as news of the fall had spread. Of course she managed it with ease and acquired a large collection of cash!

'As you go back into my husband's family history it gets very complicated. Years earlier, they had been a circus family but the circus gradually fizzled out in popularity to be replaced by the fairground. As long as I can remember we have been firmly bound up with the fairground. But it was never an easy life; children had to grow up fast. My grandfather would always tell me to smile if he saw me looking sad – you had to smile for the customers at all times. And he didn't like me mixing with people from outside the fairground; it was quite a closed society.

'There is another story of two grandfathers in the family having a fierce battle for the best pitch for the stalls and then completely forgetting their rivalry and going out for a drink together!

'I was born in Middlesbrough in 1927. My dad was an electrician, who wasn't originally from the fairground world, but my mother wouldn't dream of leaving the life. She didn't like the idea of living in houses or anything permanent and he just went along with her way of thinking. When the Second World War broke out, he went back to his

former profession, working for the engineering firm Dorman Long which later became part of British Steel. During the war an electrician was a protected occupation, but my dad still didn't manage to escape danger as he was badly burned when the factory caught fire after a bombing raid.

'Being on the fairground, like my mum I never lived in a house as a girl; I lived in a trailer. We travelled quite a bit when I got a little older. Dad kept his job on in Middlesbrough and we would travel locally round fairgrounds in nearby places like Stockton and Hartlepool. We used to have a roll a penny stall and various other stalls. It was a very happy life even if we were far from well off. As it was the only thing I had ever known, I always took living in a trailer for granted. I can remember my dad used to go back and forth to work on his motorbike from wherever we were doing a fair. The fairgrounds we used to go to then were not nearly as large or as elaborate as today. We'd maybe just about make a living, but not a fantastic living, and it was only for so many months of the year. Dad always went back to his work as an electrician when there were no fairs for us to go to.

'The outbreak of the Second World War came as a shock to everyone and the fairground world was quickly disrupted. I can remember my mum took my sister Edna and me to her parents' caravan at Crook, County Durham the night before war was declared. She was looking for somewhere safe we could go to because we knew that the fairground

business would have to come to an end – for a while, at least. We had blackout curtains in our caravans and it was all very exciting. After we had been at Crook for a while, we found a field in Catterick with a few of the other showmen in it. It was a good place for my sister and me and we were there for a good year. Later, the bombing was not as bad as before in Middlesbrough and so we went back there, which was like coming home.

'Then, as the war started to draw to a close, we began doing little bits of fairgrounds again as life slowly returned to something like normal. It was difficult because no one had any money to spare in those days. There was a holiday fair in Northallerton one night and that's where I met my future husband, Chris Edwards. I was only young – eighteen or nineteen, I think. There was a showmen's dance in the town hall and of course we girls went along for the evening. We always thought the showmen were smart and good-looking. Chris certainly was, and we hit it off straight away. He used to come over to see me wherever we went. We never seemed to be at the same fairground, but he always managed to visit me. Once I met Chris there was never anyone else for me. We courted until I was twenty and then got engaged and were married in 1948, when I was twenty-two. He was a wonderful, hard-working husband and we were very happy together.

'It was a good job my husband was so industrious. His father had died from the after-effects of the First

World War, and from then on he had to take over responsibility for looking after his mother and his younger brother and sister. The first job he went for after his dad's death was working for a farmer pulling peas, but of course the authorities soon intervened and dragged him back to school. So his mother came back to Wakefield and got a job working for British Rail. She worked there until Chris left school.

'It was later when I met him and he and his mother had decided to go travelling again. The Edwards and Johnson families used to have positions at fairgrounds. Chris went to the Showmen's Guild to claim them and the Guild made sure he got what was rightfully his. He and his mother used to have coconut shies and dart stalls, and things like that. We carried on travelling when we got married, but he still always looked after his mother; he was very caring. The only time I ever heard my husband argue with his mother was after she had put all the family photos in a brown lizard-skin bag and thrown them away when she moved from one trailer to another. He lost all of the pictures of his heritage and he was very upset. I don't think she realised how important they were to him. His mother used to be with us until her other son was old enough to take over.

'I married within the circle; that was important to me. When I met Chris, it was just perfect. We hadn't got a lot of money, but we weren't short and showmen always like big wedding ceremonies so we had a very grand wedding in St Hilda's Church, in

Middlesbrough. About four hundred people came and we all ate a cold ham salad buffet because rationing was still in force. Then we went to Dublin for our honeymoon, which was very unusual in those days. We had a brand new caravan built because we knew we had to do a lot of travelling with the fairgrounds. Chris certainly wasn't ever short of cash and I began to think he must be quite well off. But when we came back from our honeymoon, we both got quite a shock. I thought he had some money because he always looked as if he had, and he thought I had some money for exactly the same reason. Unfortunately, we were both wrong!

'After our honeymoon we realised that neither of us had much money at all. In fact, in cash we had a single Irish ten-shilling note between us! Fortunately, we had just enough in Post Office savings accounts to keep us going and we lived on a meagre £3 a week from February until Easter, when the fairground business started up again. Then we just carried on travelling.

'Chris was born in 1950. He was always a very pleasant little child. As he grew up, he became a joy – he really was a lovely little boy. We were travelling with the fairground then, but he was born at Saltburn-by-the-Sea because my mother and father had a business down there. They had some little amusements down by the seaside. I went into hospital in the town. Our first son was christened there. Young Chris was always very pleasant and

popular, a happy little lad who loved sport. As a baby, he was lovely – I remember he was a very good child from the start. Unfortunately, he was spoilt because he was the first baby we had in the family for quite a time. There was never any doubt he was going to be called Christopher after his father. If he had been a girl, he would have been called Christine! He was always going to be another Chris. I never had any hesitation about keeping the name going.

'We took our wagon down to Saltburn-by-the-Sea so I still had my own home – I wanted to be settled for the birth. My husband was at the fairground in York, so baby Chris was two or three days old before his father got home to see him. We hadn't got a car then and of course we didn't have a telephone. To speak to my husband on the phone, I used to have to go to a phone box in Saltburn-by-the-Sea at certain arranged times and he would ring me up every morning and every evening to make sure I was all right. I would go to the phone box and wait for the call.

'As a boy, Chris liked Saltburn-by-the-Sea and he still likes it today. We used to go there quite a lot to see my mum and dad; we took baby Chris back there to be christened. My sister Edna is still there. The amusement park has gone but she has a café and a fish and chip shop, and she sells candy floss. I always wanted to have children – I think everyone did in those days. From then on, my whole life changed and it was all about our son, Chris.

'Then it all changed again when it was Chris and

Laurie. Two years and ten months later, Chris's little brother came along. It seemed like a reasonable gap! We've all been together ever since. It used to be just the four of us and of course the boys were with us all the time we were working; we were all very close. Laurie is a bit different to Chris in his attitude. With Chris being the older one, he has always been in charge, the leader. When we lost his father eighteen years ago, Chris just took over being in charge of the family straight away. We have always been very close.

'I loved the fairground life, but it was far from easy. You could make a good living in the summer, but in the winter there would be no money coming in and it was often very hard. My husband, like lots of other fairground men, had to find a job. He was not a lazy man by a long way, but he absolutely hated the work he found on building sites. Although he didn't mind the hard graft itself, he loathed being all scruffy and dirty, and up to his eyes in mud. He used to complain that if it rained they would go into this shed to shelter and he could smell people's clothes and he hated it. Showmen are very particular.

'My husband stuck it out for so long and then one really wet day he came home and I could see he'd had enough. Laurie would only have been a baby in a carrycot at the time and little Chris was sitting on a chair, aged three. My husband was at the end of his tether and he just announced that he was never working on building sites again. He had made the decision and he said: "Right, even if I have to beg,

steal or borrow, I am going to earn my own living. I am determined my boys will never have to do this."

'That was when the Edwards family first went into retail and it was by no means an instant success. First, my husband started buying and selling stuff. Without any real experience or knowledge of the market that didn't work very well. Some weeks he did all right and we had money and other weeks he didn't, and money was very short indeed. Quite soon, he decided to try and make a living on the markets in the winter. In the early days it was very hard and they were quite tough times. Our lives soon became divided into fairgrounds in the summer and markets in winter. My husband was a very hard worker. My son Chris, of course, was just like his father.

'We had a stall on Wakefield Market and as a little boy, Chris used to run up from school to the market and help me close up before we could go back to the wagon and make his tea. Our first warehouse was an old body off a van. We used to sell non-ration sweets then – we would go to the potteries and buy seconds.

'In those early years of Chris's life we spent a lot of time travelling with the fairgrounds. If we could get him – and later, Laurie – into a school, then we did, but it all depended on how long we were at a fairground. We used to finish travelling in October, and the boys would go to school in the winter in Wakefield until we started travelling again at Easter. Chris went to the little Wakefield Cathedral School that was just round the corner from the market. As *he grew up, he used to be able to run up at lunchtime and would come and have a sandwich with me on the stall. He was maybe six or seven, before Laurie was at school. Of course there was no worry about anybody attacking children or anything in those days. I always used to make something on the market stall for us to have for our lunch. He would come up after school to help me pack up because my husband was always at another market. Then we went down home and I would make his tea because fortunately the caravans were not far from the market so it was handy. Our address used to be "Market Place, Wakefield" and we got our post delivered to the market office. We didn't used to do the markets in the summer then, just in the winter, because the main fairground season was Easter until October. Then, as the boys got older we thought maybe we could manage the two as there was the four of us.*

    'Laurie went to the same first school as Chris and then, when they got older and left junior school, they went to the Cathedral Secondary School – a very good secondary school. The headmaster, Mr Speke, was very, very good. He always used to keep a place for us; he knew when we would be coming back. Mr Speke was always very interested in Chris and Laurie. Once, when I came to try and get Chris in, the first response from someone else was: "Oh, we'll have to see whether he can get in. I don't think you'll be able to get in at that school." So I went down to see Mr Speke and he said: "Look, there will always

be a place for Chris and Laurie. Don't go to anyone else, just come straight to me." Rules were not as strict as they are now and he saw potential in both of the boys.

'Chris didn't do all the classes because he missed a lot of time in the summer because we weren't settled down long enough, but somehow he always seemed to keep up. We made sure the boys could both read and write. He just did ordinary schoolwork and he never had any bad reports.

'We didn't settle down in a house until after Chris got married. I think they were more innocent times, back then. Lots of the terrible things we hear about nowadays didn't seem to happen then. You could live on the "Market Place, Wakefield" and be safe. Always, we felt safe. We would travel all over the north of England and sometimes we would maybe get the boys in to a school, if it was a big fair and we were stopping for three weeks, but I don't think they really learned anything in those short bursts. Of course it's different now – the fairground children have their own education officer, and parents who take them back and forth to school.

'Unfortunately for Chris and Laurie, it was only about six months of the year when they did any schooling. Then there were the summer holidays while we were away, but we always bought them books to read, mainly storybooks and football annuals.

'I could never have imagined that my Chris would build a business the size of Poundworld. He was

bright, of course – to their mum, he and Laurie were both very special. Chris always wanted to improve things, even when he was very young. For instance, he would suddenly suggest the stall needed a fresh coat of paint to make it look smarter. He always wanted it to look better. Very early on, he realised how important it is to set your stall out as attractively as possible and he is no different now. To me he is the same Chris today as he was when he was fifteen years old and he enjoyed himself with his football. He has always had a lot of energy and the desire to work hard. We didn't ever dream of him doing anything other than the fairground business.

'But as Chris was growing up, the fairground business was becoming increasingly difficult. My husband decided we would be better off concentrating more on the markets. As I've said, he was always very hard working and he was a good father and a good husband. We didn't have a lot of money, not by a long way, but the boys always came first: we were just a team that worked very, very hard. When we used to travel, I would be driving the car or the van with the trailer behind. Laurie would be with me and Chris would be with his father in the big lorry that pulled the caravan. Touch wood, neither of them gave us any cause for anxiety. I'm not saying we used to agree about everything, but I have never known Chris answer his father or me back. His dad was strict and they were always brought up to know how to behave.

'*We've seen a lot of changes over the years. In my grandmother's day they had horses to pull their wagon, but after the war we used to have a big lorry. That's what we used to put all our equipment in and we would couple the wagon to the back of the lorry. As the boys got older, we bought them a smaller trailer so that they had a place of their own. It was a touring trailer – a caravan, we'd call it now.*

'*We combined the markets with the fairgrounds for quite a long time while the boys were growing up. I used to do all the driving before Chris passed his test. We would keep some stalls on in the summer and that meant driving very long distances. With the travelling we seemed to be working all the hours God sent but we were a great family team and we would try anything to bring in money for the family. I remember when hot dog stalls came in, I went to my husband and told him, "I'm going to get one of those." "Go away, I'm not going into food!" he said. But I talked him round and I had a hot dog stall on the markets. Young Chris used to do the market and I would mind my stall. Laurie and big Chris did the fairground business. We used to go back home every night.*'

My mother has a wonderful memory; it's much better than mine. Really, I just recall a very happy childhood. A fairground is a fantastic place to grow up in and I do feel that I was extremely fortunate. We might not have been well off, but there are the haves and the have-nots in every walk of life. When you get plenty of love and affection, you don't realise you've got very little in the way of money or material possessions. Generally, it is only as you get older that you start thinking, 'What can I do to make my family's life better?' Amazingly, in the fairground business I believe that you think about that very, very early on in life. I think by the time I was thirteen or fourteen I was really thinking, 'What can I do to improve the life of my family?'

What you did find in the fairground was that you grew up very quickly. If you were fourteen in the fairground, your mentality was much tougher and more aware than any other normal fourteen-year-old. For a while you have two lives: you go into school and you live in the normal world, then back in the fairground you are basically living an adult life. When you are in a family like ours you have to work hard and do your bit. Even when I was a kid, if any of my friends came talking to me when I was doing my job, my dad would tell them to go away in no uncertain terms. It was a grown-up world where work was concerned. The friendship and camaraderie was fantastic, though. But the best bit about growing up on the fairground was the football. Once everything was set up, we would all meet round the back for a game, men and lads together. There was enormous rivalry, but great warmth and friendship too.

Like a lot of young boys I did have ambitions to play professional football. I had trials with Leeds United when Don Revie was there – the first time was when I was fourteen. The trainer, Les Cocker, came to see me play in a showmen's game in midweek on a local pitch in Leeds. He left at half-time but not before he had approached my dad and asked me to come for a trial. I should have gone for the trial that Christmas, but I got really badly injured after Les Cocker left – I tore a muscle in my thigh and then it bled. Of course I should have come off, but I kept on playing. Towards the end I had to come off and ended up spending six weeks in hospital. I got a blood clot and the doctor prescribed bed rest so I was kept in hospital to try and get rid of it. When you're a kid you don't realise the doctors and your parents are all thinking that it could get into your system and kill you.

After four weeks the problem was not going away so the doctors decided to operate to take the blood clot out because it wouldn't dissolve. It meant that I missed out on my dream of having a trial for Leeds. But they wrote to me again, asking me to attend another trial close to Easter, the following year. I did a silly thing, really. Because I had been so confident playing football with men at fourteen, I went for that trial without playing any other games since my injury. I'd had a total of six weeks in hospital and after no more training than a kickabout with my brother, I went for the trial and I don't think I showed very well, to say the least. So that was my one and only claim to fame. It was traumatic, but you get over these things, don't you?

CHAPTER TWO

AN EDUCATION

There was a pretty rigid discipline about life when I was young. My dad was harder on us than many fathers, though not so hard as others. I don't say every kid had the same strict upbringing as Laurie and I had, but a lot of them did. Some people on the fairgrounds thought that education came first and if they could afford it, they would send their kids away to private boarding schools, but for us that was never an option.

I didn't really get on at school; I just got over it. For me it was a nuisance that I didn't need. Years later, I thought long and hard about education for my own children before all three went to private school. And it was not that I thought, 'I'm going to give them everything I never had' – I feel very comfortable in my own skin and when it comes to my education, I wouldn't change a thing. It was because when I got married,

I looked at the situation and naturally I wanted something better for my own kids than the schooling I'd had. Personally, I never thought I fell short on my education because what you miss academically, you gain by using your head quicker. I just about coped with lessons, but when you miss six months of the year you will always be behind. At school I always felt that I had missed so much they could never bring me up to date. Sometimes I felt inadequate because I was so far behind, but I compensated by throwing myself into the family business.

Every year at Wakefield I would arrive for half a year of schooling. As my mum has said, the secondary school headmaster there – Mr Speke – was very, very supportive. I don't remember much about the primary school; I don't have good memories. At secondary school I was comfortable but I never really felt that I belonged there, even though I had some good friends. I could play football so that made me lots of friends. Apart from cricket – I was never there in the summer – I did all the sports: I swam and ran for the school, I played football and rugby too. It came naturally to me and I found it very easy. Academically, I wasn't pushed. I never took any GCE O-levels because I left at fourteen.

In my last year at school I missed attending most Fridays because my dad used to take me and drop me off at Thurnscoe Market in Barnsley. He left me there to run the stall by myself at fourteen. I have vivid memories of this because to me it always seemed to be bloody cold! Dad used to go to Mexborough Market and he would drop me off on the way at 8.30am, with all my boxes of whatever I was selling at the time, which was usually crockery and other household goods and equipment. Then, at the end of the day, when he had packed up his stall, he would come round to nearby Thurnscoe and pick me up somewhere between five and six. Alone, I was dealing with customers, handling money and generally doing a man's job.

I didn't fully appreciate it at the time but even then I was being trained as a businessman. At school I never did business studies, but when you're looking after a stall, you soon learn the difference between profit and loss. It was simple: you got your money, you counted it and that was that. I just gave it to my dad and on the Monday morning, I went back to school again. I just got pocket money. I don't think I was ever academically minded, but from an early age, I knew how to run my own stall.

CHAPTER THREE

MARKETS AND ME

I can't remember a time when I wasn't determined to do whatever I did as well as I possibly could. Always, I wanted to do well. Although I knew we weren't well off, I never felt inferior to anyone else. When I was about twelve or thirteen, I remember my older cousin Clifton saying something about some people we knew who were much better off than us. He said: 'It's all right you being friends with this group of people now because you're kids, but when you get older you won't be able to afford to keep up with them.' That thought really registered with me and I deeply resented the idea. To this day, I can recall the impact it had on me. 'Ah, that's not how it's going to be with me,' I thought. From an early age I didn't fancy that description – I think it made me even more determined to do my utmost to make a go of it all. I don't think I was ever really striving for success or wealth or whatever, I was just terrified of failure and being skint! Soon afterwards what happened was that we were so determined not to fail, as well as doing the fairgrounds we started doing the markets more and more.

We would go round the travelling fairs, but we never went much further north than Newcastle. Barrow-in-Furness in Cumbria was the furthest we travelled from Wakefield. We started concentrating more on the markets. Mum and me used to do the fairgrounds and then on market days we would travel back to Wakefield and I would work on the market stall and she would work on her mobile hot dog stall. That was a bit of a fairground item but it worked on a market, mainly thanks to her amazing determination. For several years we would find ourselves travelling back to Wakefield at strange times. We wouldn't go to Newcastle on a Friday and stay over and do Saturday; instead we would come back on a Friday night and run the stall and then travel back again. Why we did that, I don't know – I wasn't old enough to influence the decision. I like to think I would have had the presence of mind to say, 'Look, it would be easier to stay overnight somewhere rather than go back and forth every Friday and Saturday.' I think my mum wanted to come back and look after my brother and my dad. She was driving because those were the days when I was not old enough to drive. My mother is quite remarkable; she always has been.

As you get on with your life you take all this early experience of hard work for granted, without thinking it's that much out of the ordinary. The stories don't come out as often as they used to with my mother, but I think I look at my past through a different pair of eyes now. I've had so many ups and downs and different experiences that I sometimes quietly wonder to myself, 'How the bloody hell did we do that?'

I think the urge to work hard and do well stems from my childhood. It wasn't so much drilled into me as being simply obvious that was the way it was: if you wanted anything, you had to work hard for it. I am definitely a product of the fairground environment – it's a world that was everything to me. I've just attended the funeral of a close friend of my brother and me from our young travelling days and it was a very moving experience. Of course it was very sad, but it was also uplifting to see so many old friends, who will always be friends because we are all fairground people. You never lose your connections with the fairground people; it's where you come from. If somebody asked me: 'Who are you?' I would say, 'Well, I'm from the fairground first. Everything else comes second, even Poundworld.' The fairground is a strong background. At the funeral I realised when I talked to the people still in it that it is still quite a closed society, but despite this it was a remarkable place to grow up.

I was twenty-one or twenty-two years old and full of enthusiasm and new ideas when I eventually left the fairground and went full-time on the markets, although I'd already been working there part-time for years. Dad was pretty tough on me because tough as I had it, my dad had had it a whole lot worse. Even though he'd always worked for himself, he never had it easy. As far as he was concerned there was only one way to do things and that was *his* way! He used to say to me: 'When it's your turn, you can do what you want; when you're working with me, you'll do as I tell you.' I think my dad's tough attitude was why, later on, I was soft on my own son and let him have his head and fulfil his dream of achieving great retail success.

There were great characters on the markets in those days. I remember a fruiterer whose nickname was Cockney Mick. He was several years older than me. Mick and I were always the first in the morning to arrive on the market. It was a massive big market and we were both keen to do as well as we could. It was hard, demanding work in all weathers. I remember Mick coming up to me and saying: 'The problem with me and you is we'll never make any real money because we are far too busy making a living.' It must have been fifty years ago but I've never forgotten that wise remark. Mick has a fruit and veg shop in Morley now and I met him recently. He's still at it. Mind you, so am I!

There were lots of memorable people around. Len Oram was another fruit and veg guy, who I used to stand next to on a Saturday. He believed in shouting up customers and from early in the morning, he would urge prospective punters on with the strange cry of: 'I won't be around tomorrow, the donkey's pissed on the strawberries!' If he said it once, he said it a hundred times a day. It was his favourite spiel and he did not have a wide repertoire. Len was a large fellow and his wife was very skinny. They were getting on in years – and not getting on at all together. All day long, they would argue. She used to throw spuds and tomatoes at him. A good man, he remained remarkably cheery considering his lot in life. Between market traders there was a feeling of camaraderie rather than rivalry because rarely was someone selling the same thing: there was a wool man, a shirt man, a fish man, and so on. We were selling housewares broadly similar to the goods we sell to this day.

I'm not sure the opportunities on markets now are what they used to be, but if anyone wants to learn how to deal with people, they're a great place to start. Markets taught me how to edge my way forward and to look at a different format every day. When I was on the market I would try lots of different ways to sell things and promote all sorts of different products to see what attracted the punters. It makes you think on your feet: you're not only dealing with the people you're buying from, you're dealing with the ones you're selling to as well. You learn about positions too. One of the things my dad taught me was the importance of location, presentation and lighting. Today, really bright lights shine in all our shops and I like to see everything smart and well presented; that started in the markets. If you can stand the weather, markets are a good place to work. I used to get up at six o'clock in the morning and my first question would always be: 'What's the weather like?'

Whatever it was like, you couldn't have a day off: you had to go to work. I used to get on the market early. Every day, I would arrive religiously at 6.45am. Where I eventually used to have my stalls there was an aisle and everybody would come in at different times, and if you were the last one there sometimes you couldn't get in and you had to carry everything. I always wanted to be there first, so my van and me were in early and when all the other people had gone, I would get my van out. Now that went on for donkey's years; I always had to be there early to beat everybody else.

Don't forget in those days you didn't start on the market in a good location. Instead you began with secondary positions that were not in the best places. You had to spend years going in and signing on the casual list. It was no fun but this is what I had to do and I did it. Whoever didn't turn up on that list provided a vacancy and then I'd get their stall. Eventually you got a full-time stall but anyone who had been on the market longer than you would be higher up in the pecking order so you've got to be on the market for several years to gain a decent position. However, I did get a bit of a jump-start in my market career because my dad used to play golf with the market superintendent! Fortunately, he made a good friend of the powerful market boss, Walter Morgan, and my mum became a good pal of his wife, Sylvia. Without a shadow of a doubt had it not been for a decision by Walter Morgan, I would not be where I am today. I owe a great debt to him and my dad.

Back then I didn't realise that my dad had set me up for such a brilliant boost. Probably the best two stalls on Wakefield Market were numbers H1 and H2. They were right by the entrance to the market hall, much better positions than I had ever had before. Of course Dad knew it was a great chance for me to do much better than I had been doing. When I went home for my tea that night he didn't actually say anything, he had simply put a sign on the window ledge, saying 'H1' and 'H2'. We were sitting down, having our tea, before I noticed. My dad had put it there on purpose; he knew the impact it would have on me. It was massive for me at that time, a huge leap forward – they were great stalls.

There had been a lot of hoo-ha about these stalls, which never seemed to come up. I was aware that for the first time in ages they were coming up, but I didn't think I stood a chance. That was where my dad's influence came in. I kept looking at the two magical numbers and eventually he said to me: 'Well, aren't you going to ask me then?' And the bottom line was the star stalls in the market were mine! That is H1 (the stall with my grandmother in the photo on Page 1 of the picture section) and next to it was H2. They were in the very best position, near where everyone came and went. For the next fourteen years, I worked there every single market day. It made all the difference between earning what felt like almost like no money to generating a lot of cash.

So, instead of struggling to earn a pretty meagre living, almost instantly I went straight to making much more money and no one appreciated this promotion more than me. I remembered how difficult it was when I used to be on the casual list, turning up and getting stuck out on a limb somewhere or even getting no stall at all. When I did eventually get myself a permanent stall it was in an obscure position but I was still glad to have it and to earn a small living. There were hundreds of stalls on Wakefield Market and because I had been on almost every one of them over the years, I knew them all well.

This was definitely one of my early lessons in the importance of who you know, as well as what you know, because quite simply, Walter Morgan changed my life. In fact, I will always believe that if you want to wind the clock back to discover why we are here today, with Poundworld successful and growing fast, then taking over the Wakefield Market stalls H1 and H2 has to be the biggest single reason. I got the opportunity to have a star billing, five or six years in advance of when I should have had it. It was brilliant! What you don't see in that picture (on Page 1 of the picture section) is that the entrance to the market is twelve feet away from my stall so it was an absolutely prime position. Everyone who came to the market came my way. It was wonderful! And it totally transformed my working life from scraping around on the fringes to a proper business with real potential. That one move probably multiplied my takings by six. From then on, I could make real money and for the first time in my life I could save money too.

I was just eighteen years old.

Wakefield Market was a big vibrant market that used to bring the town alive. It was a wonderful place to be. If you want atmosphere, there's nowhere better than a busy market. When I got there in the morning the expectation would be electrifying. Of course times change and in later years I felt that same energy slowly diminish and even disappear altogether – I don't think it's there now. But I always got a real buzz from the market and the expectation that you were going to earn your living. If you were good at what you did, you earned a good living – and if you weren't, then I'm afraid you didn't last long.

It's a competitive business, not so much with other stallholders but when it comes to creating your own identity. I had hundreds and hundreds of regular customers who all knew me by my first name. My stall became a meeting place because it was so central. People used to say: 'I'll meet you at Chris's stall.' It was also a great learning process for me. There is nothing like fairgrounds and markets to teach someone the basics of commerce. It's not a corporate learning or the sort of education you would get at university, but it does teach you about buying and selling and, best of all, about people.

The market stalls were becoming an increasingly bigger part of my life as the income from the fairgrounds steadily declined. We were still very much a fairground family at heart but it came to the point when I had to make a choice between market stalls and the fairground. I made the decision when I was twenty-one years old. I'd been working on the markets in the winter and the fairground in summer pretty much all of my life. We would tour all over the north, from Barrow-in-Furness to Sunderland, Newcastle, etc., etc., and then I would go back to the markets full-time after the summer to retain the stalls that we had. Of course to retain regular stalls you had to go back at least every four weeks and pay your back rent. I was always careful to make sure I made that trip. When I wasn't there, some casual trader would get my stall until I came back full-time.

I even used to work the Sunday markets. In my mid-twenties I did it for three summers in a village called Hunmanby, which is next door to Filey, a village on the east coast. Once, it even landed me in trouble with the law. It was before Sunday trading was legal and so I was taken to court and fined £100 and told not to do it again. I still went back the next Sunday, though.

I was grateful then for the help of my football friends, like our centre half, Gary Dobson, and Paul Tibbles, who was the goalkeeper. Often they would come to the market to help me and it was a full day. We'd meet at about five o'clock in the morning, drive all the way to the coast, spend the whole day there and then go back late at night. Sometimes we didn't make that much money so I couldn't pay them, but they used to settle for a pint of lager! That shows you what good friends they were. On Bank Holiday weekends we used to do Sunday and Monday and we would sleep in the back of the van – I couldn't afford to pay for any accommodation. We used to sell sunbeds at the market and we'd sleep on them too. It was good fun but we made very little money.

Markets are never easy, whatever day of the week you're out there.

CHAPTER FOUR

MARRYING OUTSIDE THE COMMUNITY

Decision time for me was when I made up my mind that I was going to get married. I had met someone outside the fairground community that I wanted to make my wife. As far as my family and all the fairground folk were concerned, Lorraine was a complete outsider. It doesn't matter quite so much nowadays, but back then marrying outside the community was a big thing. It had happened before in our family. My paternal grandfather had not been in the business and that marriage had worked out happily enough so it was far from unprecedented, even if it was unusual. I would say that at the time I got married eight or nine out of every ten of the fairground marriages were within the community.

When I decided to get married I was twenty-one. Back then I still had two choices of work: I could go full-time on the markets or I could go travelling with the fairground. My dad advised me very wisely, I believe. He said: 'Knowing the person you're marrying and knowing how specialised a life you have in the fairground business and how demanding that can be, I would suggest you do the markets.' He didn't think Lorraine would fit into the fairground world very well. It was a completely different world then and it would have been very difficult for someone from outside to fit in.

It's still not easy to this day, all these years later. I don't know whether the passage of time has made things any easier, but it is a special kind of person who can deal with joining the fairground family. It requires someone who can easily adapt to other people's ways. Lorraine is the mother of my three kids, although we no longer live together. Happily, we are still friends, to a point. As it turned out, she couldn't adapt, as I found out in our early days together. She used to work in an office before we were married and the world of market stalls came as a complete culture shock. I could understand how she felt. Once you step from a steady job into trying to earn your own living, the hours are never measured. It is very different from the ordered, salaried way of life.

I decided to take my dad's advice so I turned full-time on the market. He gave me the stalls I'd been running for several years. It was not a complicated negotiation, he just said: 'You do the market.' For me it was a multiple of firsts: I had never been married before, I'd never had my own home before and I'd never had my own business before. Fortunately, I still had my dad behind me.

The first house we ever had as a family was the one I bought. It was 1972 and I was twenty-two, taking on the market full-time and stopping the fairground side. I was going to get married and I needed some accommodation. At first I didn't know what to do. I had no money to speak of because I'd always worked for my dad. All he'd ever given me was a wage, but that was just money to spend on myself; I had no other commitments. So I set out to find a house in Wakefield. Eventually I found a seven- or eight-year-old semi-detached house on an estate. After living all my life in wagons and caravans it felt very strange, but I knew Lorraine had to have a house. It cost £3,750. My dad, bless him, gave me £1,000 towards the deposit and I got a £3,000 mortgage and put £750 down on the house. My mortgage repayments at that time were £20 a month. The figures do not seem large now but it was the first debt I'd ever had and I think for a while I was in shock.

My only transport was a Ford Escort van, which doubled as a car. I think the stress that I took on with everything being new sent me into a state of numbness – somehow I just had to narrow my options down, I felt. At the end of the day there was a need for money so I think I closed everything down and gave myself something to focus on. More than ever before, money became increasingly prominent in my thoughts because up to the age of twenty-one when I was doing the market, I was always working with my dad. As I've said, he used to go to his own market, dropping me off on the way, and I went to mine. Before I got married I was always living at home so I had no real stress in any way.

Buying a property was a big thing. It was very different for me but I had a wife who was used to living in a house. She must have seen something in me, I suppose, but it was very strange for her when she took me back to her parents' house to meet them and I took her back to our trailer to meet mine. I can't remember much anxiety over that, though. I met Lorraine at a works Christmas do – I used to play for local football teams and I had no problem gelling with the lads who played football. Our backgrounds may have been different but the common denominator was always football. As long as you could play football, you could mix with anybody. I was in with a good bunch of lads, most of whom I am still friends with today, and I was full of confidence, especially on the football pitch. Off the pitch, I was not so sure of myself.

As I've said, Lorraine used to work in an office. I was eighteen when we met and it was my first serious relationship. The fact was of course that I had been living quite a sheltered life under my parents' wings in a very comfortable and safe environment. If I'm honest, I was not at all mature about the ways of the world and relationships – I was eighteen going on ten, really.

I remember the moment I was sitting outside on a step on the morning we were getting married. Although I was still feeling the after-effects of the night before, there was much more than that on my mind. Marriage and a whole new way of life seemed to be happening so fast; there was no elaborate preparation. People now plan expensive stag and hen dos that take place all week long, all over the world, but not in my day. In any case, I couldn't have afforded that: it was just a few drinks on the night before the wedding. I remember a few friends turned up and we went into Wakefield, then I felt very ill on the morning of the ceremony. So there I was, sitting on the bottom step, waiting to put on my suit. I was bent over, looking none too bright, and my dad walked past and asked me if I was all right.

'No,' I said, 'I feel terrible!'

But he showed me no mercy and proceeded to say something to me that I have never forgotten. He said: 'It's not as bad as you're gonna feel.' And then he paused and added: 'After this day, your life will never be your own.' Very quickly, I realised over the following years exactly what he meant, as we all do as we get older and, hopefully, wiser. You think you know it all when you're young and it's, 'Oh, bring it on!' In fact, as time moves on, you realise you know virtually nothing.

Dad was quite a strong character. As far as my marriage was concerned, his attitude was: 'I'll help you where I can, but it's up to you.' My parents may have been upset because I was marrying out of the business but if they were then they kept it to themselves. To be honest, I can understand why my marriage may have gone off on the wrong foot. We decided against having a honeymoon because we couldn't afford it, so that was one step towards disaster. For us there were no luxurious holidays: we couldn't afford New York, or even Spain at the start. So we had just the one night in the hotel; we couldn't even manage a week in Scarborough or Blackpool.

We had quite a big reception and the England football team just happened to be playing around the time of the function. It was on television so all my friends decided they were going to watch the match. There was a TV in a lounge near the function room and I just happened to be walking past and thought, 'I wonder how they're doing?' So I went in and looked over to the screen at the precise moment my wife in her wedding dress just happened to be walking past! Lack of honeymoon was the first mistake, though you can't do what you can't afford, and watching football proved to be the second. The third and final mistake was not being able to switch off from work, even on such an important day.

I had a van full of stock, which represented my whole livelihood, parked in town outside the hotel in Wakefield, where we spent our wedding night. The only vehicle I possessed, it also held most of my worldly goods and our future together, so I was not at all relaxed. Every half hour or so, I kept waking up and looking out the window to make sure it was still there and no one had pinched it. My only excuse was that my whole life revolved round what I was selling: my stock. I think my actions were practical, though definitely not very romantic. And the next day after the wedding, I went to work on the market as usual.

That is why anyone in my business, and there are a lot of us out there, has Del Boy from the BBC's *Only Fools and Horses* as a permanent reminder of what life in the market world is really like. The person who put that brilliant programme together really understands the life of a market trader. It's so well written and expertly acted. Del Boy and his team all seem to know how often comedy and tragedy always hang delicately in the balance.

On my wedding day I was also a little preoccupied because our house purchase hadn't quite gone through, so we were forced to make do and mend while the vendors sorted things out. There was a gap of about four or five weeks and so, believe it or not, we borrowed a touring trailer from a cousin of mine to live in temporarily. That was the cheapest option and we had to live there for the first five weeks after we were married while we waited to get into our house. Of course it was another black mark.

We were both under pressure. The thought of having the responsibility of marriage hung over me. I've never found it easy to relax but this was a particularly difficult time. Throughout my life I've always felt there was something driving me on and at that time I felt it more keenly than ever before. My fear of having no money, which is always with me, was more intense than ever. I've never had a life where I've had nothing; I've always had enough to get by on, but now I felt I had to put in more effort than ever before. Trying harder is what you do if you're on the market but I think even the customers found it strange that I was back on the stall the day after my wedding. 'Didn't you get married yesterday?' they were saying. Although I didn't see it as that unusual, a lot of people did. In retrospect, I was probably pushing the boat out a little too far in wanting to rush back to work to achieve and consolidate rather than take the easy option.

Also, to be frank, my parents always had a somewhat uneasy relationship with my wife, Lorraine. It was never totally settled – I think my mother and father adapted to her attitude rather than the other way round. Lorraine has quite a strong character. She is a good person and she did a great job in bringing the children up: first, with our two daughters and then later with our son, Christopher. Nicola was born first and when my wife later became pregnant with our second child, I was convinced it would be a boy – I think I wanted a footballer, a lad to play football with. For me the disappointment when a baby girl arrived lasted about ten seconds, but I don't think my wife has ever forgotten my initial feeling. Our second daughter, Sonya, and I laugh about it now. Of course, we later had a son when Christopher was born and I don't think he's ever kicked a football in his life!

We're very lucky with our children; they're all great. I've probably had more to do with our son in recent years as he has come into the business. Lorraine was never less than 100 per cent behind all the kids and I think my parents started to respect her for that. Much later, when Sonya and Nicola started their Beauty Mill business, she worked well with them for thirteen years.

My mother is eighty-eight now but most days she still comes into Poundworld to look after me, Laurie and Christopher in the morning and then she will go on to our daughters' business to help them. Family is everything to her, and it always has been. My wife had a very different upbringing from mine. Her mother died when she was quite young so she didn't know what it was like to grow up in a big family like ours. Nevertheless, she is still very close to our children.

Those early years in the marriage were not easy. Desperate to make a success of my stalls, I was working all hours and I found that I missed something of the old travelling life. I felt very isolated when the fairgrounds were going on without me. All my life I'd been used to travelling around and then I suddenly found myself stuck in Wakefield every single day.

It also felt strange being the first one in the family to buy a house; that was a huge change. Then there was a clash between home and work, where my wife was concerned. I'm sure I worked too hard and was not easy to live with, but I was doing something for the first time and she was doing the same. Each of us got over it in our own way but there were a few troubles along the way. I had a one-track mind, especially after the children arrived. They were wonderful, and they still are – I was so pleased I'd got them – but it was a stressful way to earn a living, even then. There was no wage packet on a Friday. If you haven't sold enough, you don't earn enough. If you have a bad week and it pours down every day, it's uncomfortable but then at least you do sell lots of umbrellas! It's not a normal, relaxed happy life.

I just took over the stall when I married and it became my business. Lorraine gave up work when Nicola was born.

CHAPTER FIVE

NEIGHBOURS

After we'd been living in our semi for around two years I came home one day and discovered the detached house next door had come up for sale. I thought my mum and dad might be interested in buying it. Times were changing for fairground folk and I knew that they had been considering the idea of following me from the travelling life into the home-buying world. It was a great chance to reunite the family now that a house in the same cul-de-sac was up for sale, I thought. I was absolutely delighted when my parents liked the idea and moved in. It was brilliant! There was even a shared drive to park our vehicles in.

It seems incredible now, but at the time I never thought for one moment that Lorraine might not be totally overjoyed by the idea of her in-laws living so close. Strangely, she did not share my joy at the move. I'm not saying she was 100 per cent upset, though: she never freaked out and hung from the ceiling and said, 'I'm not going to live here if they're coming!' She just had a bit of a mood on, as women do from time to time. With hindsight, it was perhaps not the most tactful move in the whole world, but it lasted from 1974 until 1980 and most of us, certainly Nicola, Sonya and me, were happy with the reunion.

My mother was certainly thrilled about the move, but I'll let her explain:

'We had been looking for a house ourselves, but we hadn't found anything suitable so we had sort of shelved the idea. But then after Chris got married, he sort of came up to his dad, and said, "The house next to me is for sale. If you buy it, we could use all the space between the two houses." There was a big area where we could put the market vans and other stuff we had. But of course at first my husband said, "Oh no, we're not going to go down there! We will be much too near you when you are just married." He was dead against the plan. Chris and Lorraine needed some space with Nicola, who was a little baby then, he said.

'I was horrified by his decision – I loved the idea of all the family being close together and I always have. I didn't often argue with my husband on anything but this time I really put my foot down. I said, "Well, if I can't go in that house, I don't want to have a house at all." I could always be awkward when I

wanted to be. And we did go in that house and we lived next to him for seven years!

'*We all got on really well, most of the time. We did ask Lorraine if she minded us coming down and she said no. We didn't live with them and we always tried not to get on top of them. In fact, I think they used to come more into our house than we did into their place – we were very handy for babysitting! Chris and Lorraine had their second daughter, Sonya, and the girls used to come into our place just as if it was their own home. Sonya took her first steps from their front door to our front door. We were all a very close family. I used to spoil the girls rotten and later, I also became very close to my third grandson, also called Chris.*

'*We are all still very tightly-knit today.*'

CHAPTER SIX

FROM STALL TO STORE

I had always had a dream of opening a shop. By the time I was in my mid-twenties I'd been working on the market for ten years full-time, and for many years before that when I was still at school. I never minded the hard work and I loved the interaction with my customers and the relative simplicity of the retail world: I bought things and I sold them. That hasn't really changed throughout my life. But while I will always have great fondness for the warmth and wit of the market world, something I appreciated even when I was very young, I yearned to move onwards and upwards with my own shop. It seemed like the natural progression, but first I had to make the money to make the considerable leap from stall to store.

Anybody in business will always tell you that the first chunk of money is the hardest to make. It is never easy to stop spending those precious initial savings on personal needs, especially when you have a wife and a growing family. I can't remember a time in my childhood and youth when I was not going to the market. If you really want to get on, it's an all-consuming daily challenge. You don't have much time to do anything else as your life is all about buying and selling. Mine certainly was, and I think that experience stands this business in good stead now. At first under my father's guidance, and later alone, I learned how to talk to people and how to gain their trust and respect. Over the years on Wakefield Market I had hundreds and hundreds of regular customers. I think they came because I was a pleasant young lad who was trying to sell something that gave value for money; I wasn't trying to pinch anybody's money, my goods were genuine and so was I.

Over the years I came to love my regular customers and to learn a lot about their needs. Many people I met on the other side on the stall became my friends and a huge part of my life. I used to do the same stalls every Monday, Thursday, Friday and Saturday. Often people would buy something just as I was packing up on a Friday and then they'd come back at 8.30 on the Saturday morning and say: 'Have you been here all night?' I hadn't, although it sometimes felt as though I had. In fact, I had packed up, gone home, eaten, slept, come out, set up and was back in the same place! It was hard work and nine times out of ten it's also cold work, and often wet work as well. Looking back, I don't know how I did it.

Through those years of my youth, I kept my dream alive. It's not easy to save money when you have a growing family and a mortgage to pay but I did everything I could to accumulate enough cash to make my dream come true. Having a shop of my own was always my ambition. All the while I kept thinking, 'One day I'm going to have a shop, one day I'm going to have a shop.' I think it was after living through nine years of penny-pinching, trying to keep enough money in my pocket to look after my wife and two kids, and still save enough to realise that ambition, that my chance came.

Out of the blue I saw a shop in Wakefield advertised for rent. And it wasn't through the normal agents. Instead the landlord was the local authority, at that time known for being a bit of a softer deal-maker than a proper commercial landlord. So I saw the shop and decided to make an offer of £100 a week for rent and rates. I told my dad and said I was going to offer for the rent. His reaction was: 'You're already doing so well with your stall, why on earth do you want a shop with rent and rates to pay?' I just said it seemed the most obvious thing to do. But I wasn't answering him back – I never did that, in fact I rarely argued with him about anything. Usually I took his advice. Anyway, I made my offer of £100 a week through a local agent (I did everything weekly, I couldn't do per annum – I wanted to know where I was every week). And I got it! My offer was accepted.

At that time my precious funds were kept in a tin box at home. I had saved and saved, and by 1975, I had got it up to around £8,000 – more than twice the cost of our house. It was a lot of money in those days. Obsessed by saving, I had the money all in cash. Before I finally found the one in Wakefield, I had looked at no end of shops. I knew nothing at all about borrowing money because I'd been brought up never to borrow anything. My capital was enough to stock the shop initially, but only just, I reckoned. Yet I knew I needed to put a new shop front on this shop to really make it work. I realised that after I had made the offer and that made my cash seem very limited – I didn't know how much that shop front was going to cost me. Here, I drew again on help from my footballing friends. One of our fullbacks, Kevin McIlroy, was an architect and he drew up the plans for me for free, or perhaps I at least bought him a pint. It turned into a team effort because Gary Dobson, the centre half, was the electrician I used and his helper was Paul Tibbles, the goalie. Basically, I got all my pals in to help. All three of them were to help me out lots of times. Then I got a quote from the shop fitter, and it was still going to cost me £2,500 to do the improvements I wanted.

I had never wanted to have a loan or an overdraft but I realised I was going to have to break my 'no-borrowing' rule almost as soon as I started. Directly across the road from the shop I was buying was the NatWest, which was my personal bank, so that seemed a suitable place to begin. So I went in and asked to see the manager, a distinguished gentleman called Mr Shackleton. I explained that I needed money to pay for the shop front. 'Where's the shop?' he asked. You could actually see it out of his office window. I said: 'It's just there.' He smiled and responded: 'That's a very good location.' I explained how much I was paying for rent and rates. 'What about stock?' he asked. 'Don't worry about the stock,' I said. 'I've got the money.' 'It's not in our bank!' he said. I explained that I hadn't got it in his bank, but that I had it at home.

'Will you show me?' he asked. This was an old school of bank manager speaking, I'm sure it wouldn't happen now. So I agreed. 'Where do you live?' asked Mr Shackleton. Very soon we were heading off to 7 Kingsway, my semi-detached home. We drove down there, I showed him the contents of my tin box and said: 'That's going to fill that shop.' He looked at me and said quietly: 'You've got your money.'

Although I put the shop front in as quickly as possible, that led to the next major problem. I was doing the shop fit-out in my spare time, but while installing my racking, I suddenly thought to myself, 'This is crazy, I'm doing so many things I've forgotten the obvious.' I had no one to manage the shop! As luck would have it, Dad was back from his travelling fairgrounds and just happened to be in Wakefield for two weeks because there were gaps in the schedule. That meant my brother was free as well. So Laurie said he would come and help me: 'Just for a couple of weeks, if you want!'

The timing was so fortunate I could hardly believe it. By the time he said that, I had already opened the first weekend and persuaded my wife to go into the shop with an assistant we'd managed to find. We had no idea whether we were going to be busy or quiet, or whatever. Our daughter Nicola had been born on 16 October 1972 and she was by then a baby in a pram, so Lorraine had to take her with her to work! That did not work out very well and the deal did not last long. I soon realised this was another bad move, so Laurie agreed to work there for two weeks.

After the initial two weeks my brother decided to come to the rescue for a little longer. In fact, we went on to work together for another forty years and he's only just retired! I think the whole fairground world was just starting to fade a little. Laurie was getting a little older and he found he liked working in the shop. My brother said to me how much he had enjoyed working inside, out of the weather. He then told our dad that he wouldn't mind working with me. Dad came up to me and said: 'Look, I don't know how much this shop has cost you, but I don't think it's right in my world for one son to work for another. If I pay you half of what that shop's cost, can he be a partner? Is that all right with you?'

Desperate because I knew if Laurie went off again, I had no one to run the shop, I agreed. Laurie started in 1975, but I refused to accept any cash from my dad. Instead he waited until we made the first profits from the shop and took less money than me from that. From that day onwards Laurie was with me all the way and he never left until very recently, when he retired. He agreed to the partnership and we were partners as well as brothers all our working lives. And that is how easily we came together; it was no more complicated than that.

We started off with one shop, which was an awful long way from the Poundworld of today. I called the shop Bargain Centre, and I let Laurie run it while I continued to work in the market. Life on the market was hard work: the long hours were relentless and the demands of the job meant my wife was left to bring up our two daughters on her own quite a lot of the time. But the financial rewards of having stalls in those prime positions at Wakefield Market were considerable and now I had the town centre shop, I stood a better chance of a brighter future. My brother Laurie was doing a great job and for the first time I felt that perhaps I really was going to be successful. Lorraine was pleased to be able to concentrate on bringing the children up.

Exactly how successful I was becoming came home to me in June 1976, when that great footballer Tony Currie was transferred from Sheffield United to my team, Leeds United. He was a fine player so I was delighted by the move. I was happy to see a talented new addition arrive to join Leeds, but shocked when I read in the local paper that he was to be paid £500 a week.

I thought to myself, 'I can't afford to play for Leeds any more!' By then I earned more than that. It was not a lot more, but it was more all the same. I had established the stalls and built up all my regular customers and the shop was already looking promising. My own faint thoughts of a career as a professional footballer completely disappeared: I simply wouldn't get paid enough. I wouldn't say that now!

Of course once I had successfully launched a first shop, I was keen to open another but it was very difficult to find a suitable place. In those days, high streets were profitable places and landlords preferred to rent to big corporate chains rather than individual discounters like ourselves. We searched long and hard for a couple of years and it was very frustrating that we could not discover any new openings.

For some time Laurie used to run the shop and I would work in the market. I used to buy all the stock during the week and the business was going well, but I knew that it had to grow: we needed to be bigger to get better prices from the wholesalers and to compete in the long term.

It was very hard but then we got a lucky break. Laurie decided to get married, which was probably five years after the shop opened. He went to Bradford to buy his wedding suit and he had to visit the town centre. It was the time when they were building the Arndale Centre and there was a lot of building going on all over the place. Laurie saw this very old shop, just facing where the escalator would soon be coming out of the Arndale Centre. He came back and said to me: 'I've just seen a great shop in Bradford. It would be perfect if we're going to do another shop.'

I went over to have a look and he was right; because all the main traders in Bradford were moving into the Arndale Centre, they were leaving a lot of gaps. It might have looked a bit sparse on Kirkgate, but as Laurie said, because this escalator brought people out of the Arndale Centre, it was a bright spot. So I made enquiries and found that the owners wanted £80,000 for the long leasehold. It ran until 2045 and the peppercorn rent, as they call it, was £90 a week. We managed to get the price down to £60,000 and twenty-three years later, we sold it for £900,000! That money was the cash I used to kickstart the Poundworld operation.

It looked like a good deal from the start, but the whole shop needed doing up. I was still dealing with Mr Shackleton, and by this time I had paid him his money back from the first shop. Every time he saw me in the bank he would say: 'Don't forget, if you ever want to do anything else, let me know.' I had gained his confidence, but not in ten minutes because this was a few years later. So I asked for an appointment to see him. I said that this was a bit of a different deal: it was £80,000 that I needed, and this was in 1980 when that was an awful lot of money. It was like asking for half a million quid today! Mr Shackleton seemed a little surprised. After I had picked him up and sat him back down on his chair, I said: 'There is a good side to that. They want £80,000 but I have offered them £60,000. And they've said they'll take it.'

He said: 'Will you show me?' It was exactly like taking him to see my tin box of money all over again. My advantage this time was that he knew me by now. I still did my shop banking in his branch and he knew that I had done as I'd said I would do. In my experience at that time if you did what you said you were going to do, you never had a problem with banks. If you messed about and went over on your overdraft then you didn't get another chance. So I took Mr Shackleton over to Bradford, so again he could see for himself the shop I wanted him to help me buy. It did not look too impressive a prospect at first – all boarded up, and with a big old-fashioned aisle of windows to walk through before you reached the entrance to the shop. Inside it was all in darkness as there was no electricity so we opened the door to try and let the daylight in to show us where we were going.

We've got a great many more shops now, and I have lost count of the ones I've looked at over the years, but the vital visit to this one shop still stands out in my memory. I think it was very significant for us: it was a huge shop. Upstairs was 3,000 square feet of space, while downstairs was even larger, with more than 5,000 square feet. I knew that this represented an amazing retail opportunity and I had explained it all to Mr Shackleton. Naturally, he still wanted to see inside for himself. It was not easy because it was all in darkness – the shop had been closed for who knows how many months or years or whatever. We set out to try and feel our way downstairs. Unfortunately, I'd forgotten to bring a torch and he was in front of me. I said: 'The staircase turns as you go down...' But all I heard in reply was: '*Splosh!*' The whole basement was under two feet of water and he'd put both feet in it! So I said: 'I'm really, really sorry, Mr Shackleton. I didn't realise it was flooded, I've never really looked down there.' He didn't make much of a reply. It was only when we were getting back in the car that he said: 'You've got your money.'

That £60,000 enabled me to move the shop business to another level, but the size of that debt to the bank hung very heavily over my head. By this time I was twenty-nine years old and I became obsessed by the desire to get it repaid. I did it as quickly as I could, in about five years, and when I had achieved that I felt an enormous sense of relief. The new Bradford shop turned out to be a very good investment. A much bigger place than the Wakefield shop, it was full of potential.

Of course with every new development came new problems. With my brother still in charge of Wakefield and me still enjoying the fresh air of the market, we employed a manager to run the Bradford store. In the early days at Bradford there were problems with staff dishonesty, but the shop was showing promise and clearly had great potential. My gut feeling at the time was that if all else failed, I still had a profitable market stall. While the stall existed, I knew that I too could exist because I could go back to square one and survive on my stall.

But we continued to have trouble as money kept going missing from the Bradford shop. For a while I left it going like that, with someone else keeping an eye on it for me in a loose sort of way, but gradually my feelings against the person who was stealing from me grew stronger. Strangely, I can recall in detail how I stopped going to the market and finally took action. One morning when I was heading for Wakefield Market it was raining. I got to a roundabout just near the market and I thought to myself, 'The dishonest member of staff in Bradford is probably pinching more than I can earn on the market.' Then I thought maybe I shouldn't rock the boat. I couldn't make my mind up what to do – it was just like that Chevy Chase film as I went round and round the roundabout, trying to decide which way to go. Should I carry on to my stall in Wakefield Market or should I head for Bradford to confront a staff member I was convinced was a thief? After I had travelled three times round the roundabout, I bit the bullet and set off for Bradford to sort the situation out. I removed the rotten apple and of course the Bradford shop went from strength to strength.

And that was the day when I stopped going to the market for good, although I still had the stalls – at that time you couldn't sell them but they were still a valuable asset so I got someone in to run the stalls for me. They were so close to my heart, I really didn't want to give them up. I hung on for a while but after about two years, I finally gave the stalls up – but by then I had opened a third shop in Barnsley.

The Bradford shop was the one that made the most difference to the business. It was enormous! We soon realised our stock wouldn't fill it all and so, after we finally had all the water pumped out of the big basement and had it thoroughly dried out, we rented the space out to other people. First, I suggested to my mum that she should open a café in the back of the shop. There was a separate level halfway down, where she opened a snack and coffee bar. Then I went back to a lot of my old market trader friends and made them an offer: I said I was opening this shop upstairs and directly under the top floor, I was opening a toy area. I offered units to rent in the yawning basement; I said I wanted £100 a week for these units. I soon got six or seven people interested and we started rented space. The way I looked at it, I was paying £90 a week for the rent and I was getting a lot more than that a week from my basement! Most important, of course, I was paying my debt off. I got lots of people renting space there. Some lasted a couple of years and one market trader in particular, John Ross, was there for nine years! In fact, two or three of them stayed and as the others dropped off, I didn't look to replace them with anyone else because we were doing so well in the shop that I started taking areas back.

This was great; it was like a new business. The third shop was in Barnsley and for many years, we did really well with just those three shops. They were all trading as Bargain Centre. Of course there was no comparison to the size we are now, but I realised I was doing really well in terms of measuring my wages against the friends I played football with. All the time I was always conscious the rent quarter was just round the corner and the wages bill was growing but Laurie and I worked very hard and we always tried to keep costs down. I used to do all the buying myself, from wholesalers in Manchester and in Leeds. At that time the opportunity of importing from the Far East ourselves was years away in the future.

I had learned that you've got to tread carefully. You've always got to watch what you're doing because the money is always an issue; you've got to be cautious with every move you make. But behind all that the whole motivation was clear: I've got a family and they can't go short. My brother Laurie was in a slightly different position. He was still single and didn't get married until quite a while later. When he did, his thoughts were the same as mine. We were both determined to succeed for our families. And one great advantage of working with my brother was that there was 100 per cent trust between us. Fortunately, with the Bradford shop doing particularly well, business was good. Then I ventured into a completely new area.

CHAPTER SEVEN

NIGHTCLUBS

My son Christopher has had a huge impact on my life and on the success of Poundworld. He is a remarkable young man, who has inherited my drive and determination and a few of the other qualities as well! Working closely together is not always easy, but it is always interesting. He has done so much to help make Poundworld what it is today. I know I couldn't have done it without him, but perhaps the most remarkable thing about his impact on my life is that it began even before he was born.

My wife Lorraine was pregnant with Christopher some thirty-two years ago when a good friend of mine called John Jones told me: 'We're going on holiday to America.' He knew holidays had hardly ever featured in my life until then. My first holiday was when Nicola was about two and we went to Jersey and I thought we'd flown to the other end of the world! My second holiday was a couple of years later when the three of us went with my mum and dad to Majorca. As a young man I was anything but well travelled; I never had time to take holidays. I'd not even taken a night in a B&B in Blackpool because I had always been far too busy working.

My friend knew that I had always had a dream of visiting the United States and he and his wife were planning a tremendous two-and-a-half-week round trip to Los Angeles, San Francisco, Hawaii and Las Vegas and they asked us to go with them. Even though Lorraine was expecting, we decided we would go. She promised she could tackle it and wouldn't be sick!

The only memories I have from a wonderful, eye-opening holiday are good, apart from experiencing jet lag for the first time. It was not quite so easy for poor Lorraine. We used to hire cars every place we went. Many women experience some unusual emotions when they are pregnant and my wife's was that she simply couldn't stand the smell of leather. Because of her condition, it made her feel sick. It was unfortunate for her and we had to go into every car hire place and say: 'Has your car got leather seats?' They would smile and say: 'Oh, yes!' And we'd have to say: 'I'm sorry, in that case we can't take it.' They thought we were crackers.

In spite of that we really enjoyed our time away. I liked pretty well all that I saw of America, but the place I totally fell in love with was Las Vegas. A friend asked me after I came home: 'What is Vegas really like?' 'It's like the centre of the universe,' I said. I was completely blown away by the fantastic energy of Las Vegas. The flashing lights, the masses of people and the endless razzmatazz really reminded me of my childhood days in the fairground, only it was about a hundred times more exciting. The weekend in Vegas clearly turned my head; it made a huge impression on me. I saw Tom Jones singing live; I saw Frank Sinatra singing live! It was like a surprise introduction to an exciting new world.

What happened next was something that seemed it was simply meant to be. I had only just returned home from Vegas when my brother Laurie rang me with a problem. The next day was a Sunday and he was supposed to be taking his son to a football match at the same time as a joiner was calling at the Bradford shop to repair some stairs near the entrance. The wood underneath was rotten and it clearly needed sorting out before one of our customers put a foot through it. He said the joiner was arriving at 10am on Sunday morning. 'Sorry, I know you have just come back from your holiday, but will you drive over and let him in?' he asked.

'No problem,' I said. So I drove over to Bradford and asked the joiner how long he was going to be. He said the job would take a couple of hours. I was still a bit jet-lagged and so I sat down with some time to kill. By chance there was a copy of the *Yorkshire Post* under the counter. I was idly turning the pages until I saw a little advert in the business section that said, 'Nightclub complex for sale, Halifax'. Now I'm not saying alarm bells were ringing in my head, but the advert certainly caught my attention and made me sit up and take notice.

I had only been to Halifax once before in my life, even though it was only ten or fifteen miles away. When the joiner had finished, I thought to myself that my dinner wouldn't be ready for about an hour so I decided I could get to Halifax in an hour, have a look at this place and be back in time. I shot straight over and found the nightclub building. When I got there I found that the back doors were wide open. I thought that was a bit strange, but I just wandered in. There was nobody around and then I heard somebody clattering about down in the cellar. It was a complex, rambling place and I poked around, exploring. Eventually I met up with Ida, the cleaner, who seemed to be the only person around.

She was a Polish lady, who was very helpful. I asked her who was in charge. 'It's Kevin. He will be upstairs in his flat, fast asleep. You won't wake him up. They've been working late until at least three o'clock in the morning,' she told me. The place smelt as if it had been busy; it gave me a funny feeling that was very appealing. They called it Foggy's at the time after the nickname of the owner, rugby league star Terry Fogerty. Ida gave me Kevin's number. I rang him later and said: 'I've seen your advert in the paper. I've been in and met your cleaner, I would like to meet you.'

When we eventually met, I could tell straight away that Kevin Quill was quite a character. A big, strong lad, he looked as though he could handle himself. He was an unusual guy, only about eighteen years old but with a quiet confidence. He finished up working for me for many years. We were to get on very well together, but he was initially more than a little suspicious of this stranger who wanted to buy the club he ran. Happily for me, it seemed my new car had charmed him!

At the time I had just traded in my old Jaguar XJS to get my first brand new one. Kevin was a lad who was clearly impressionable and I had turned up in a brand new shining motor. He spotted the car and clearly fell for it. I could tell he did not love it begrudgingly but genuinely appreciated a nice motor. 'Do you want to go and meet Foggy?' he asked. So I did. Foggy was the freeholder of the nightclub and we quickly did a deal. In four or five weeks after coming back from Vegas I had discovered a nightclub and bought the bloody place! I had decided I was going to recreate Las Vegas in Halifax.

Travel really opened my mind. You just think: 'Wow!' So I visited Caesars Palace in Las Vegas and I ended up buying Foggy's in Halifax! That's quite a leap. The idea of opening a nightclub had never really occurred to me before but I saw how people could be managed and entertained and just got the most amazing buzz out of watching them enjoy themselves. I was thirty-two years old and as a young kid I had been in loads and loads of nightclubs, but I had never ever thought of owning and running one of my own. I think I was really inspired by Vegas; the place simply amazed me. I was astonished by the enormous shopping malls, which didn't exist in this country at that time. The environment was just so colourful compared to the then grey places like Barnsley, Wakefield, Leeds and Bradford that I was working in. Now of course everything has lifted – Leeds, for instance, is a fantastic city – but back then comparing America to England was like chalk and cheese.

Chance plays a huge part in everything. If I hadn't been stuck in Bradford that day, I would never have gone to Halifax. But I didn't tell anyone; I just got on with it. Foggy wanted just over £200,000 for the place and in 1982 that was a huge amount of money. I didn't have £200,000, but he had connections with the brewery and so he introduced me to the guy who could arrange loans. Breweries lend money to people who are going to sell lots of their beer, I learned. I managed to negotiate the price down to £190,000 and one way or another somehow I managed to cobble the money together.

I wanted to bring some life and colour to my new project and so I really threw myself into bringing it bang up to date. Fortunately, it ended up being very, very successful. I made a great number of changes and a lot of big improvements – I had a friend who had done something similar, so it wasn't entirely my own ideas. For inspiration, I went back to my childhood in the fairgrounds. So I renamed the nightclub the Carousel and I put fairground memorabilia, like jumping horses, all around the place. I had it designed with a strong fairground theme. It looked great and that was just perfect for me: after all, the fairground is all about entertainment. Altogether, I had that building for nine years. I ran it as the Carousel for about five or six years very, very successfully. But it was not easy – I used to go over there every Friday and Saturday and two or three nights in the week as well. Kevin was running it, but I always wanted to keep a close eye on what was going on.

I didn't realise when I first met him that Kevin was the youngest member of an infamous family of four brothers and two sisters. They had a well-earned reputation and everybody in Halifax referred to the family as 'them Quills'. But I got on very well with Kevin. We had our moments, as you do in any kind of business, but I had no issues with him. His family was quite another matter, though. Even Kevin used to say: 'You know what "them Quills" are like!' In his own way, he was also an achiever; he wanted to do well, he didn't just want to be defined as one of 'them Quills'. At one point we employed a couple of his brothers as doormen too.

I think because I was always a bit fresh-faced and youthful-looking, some people felt sorry for me. At thirty-two, I probably looked more like twenty-two. People used to think, 'Poor lad, it's like a lamb to the slaughter.' But I don't think they realised that, although I looked young, I had a lot going on inside me that didn't show on my face. It probably led to them thinking I could be suckered or bullied, but I never was. When I finally sold the Carousel none of 'them Quills', not even Kevin, was there. By then he had moved on to something else. I would never criticise Kevin: he was good for me, and I was good for him, I think. And it brought me some very strange experiences.

At first, when Kevin was away on holiday, I would have to run the Carousel myself. Sometimes I'd be so busy, I'd miss a meal and many times on a night I used to find myself really hungry. In pubs and clubs the spirits are always locked away; beers are kept in the cellar and spirits are in the spirit cupboard, which in this case was in the kitchen in the flat above. One night I was rushing in to the flat to get some change out of the safe and I spotted this cake in the cupboard. I was starving so I cut myself a slice and ate it. It said '21' on top and had been partly eaten so I thought it would be OK. Soon afterwards I had an awful stomach-ache. I felt bad for four or five days and I began to blame the cake for upsetting me. When Kevin came back, he asked me if everything had been all right. So I told him it was OK, but I'd been poorly – 'I think that twenty-first birthday cake of yours might have upset me,' I added. He looked shocked and said: 'I'm twenty-two now!' He'd left it there for a whole year in his apartment and never bothered shifting it. The white icing on top hid the contents of the cake and I was sick as a dog.

Tragedy struck Kevin one night when he went out in his car and there was an accident and a young girl was badly injured. Tragically, she later died. It was a terrible time. I was lying in bed at 3am when I got the phone call in the early hours so I had to shoot over to the police station. They asked me if I could sort him out. Well, Kevin was a big lad and he was angry about what had happened. I picked him up and tried to calm him down. He wanted to go back to the club where the apartment was, but I realised he was incapable of looking after himself because he had been sedated; he was in shock. I'm surprised they passed him on to me so easily; perhaps he insisted.

Anyway, Kevin had a very strong mother. I never got on with her particularly well, but I said to him: 'Kevin, you can't stay in here because you're all by yourself.' He got very angry and he was looking to have a go at me. Kevin's brother, John Quill, was a doorman then and I was trying to send Kevin up in a cab to his mother's house. Kevin tried to make a grab for me and I pushed him away and his brother John came in and said: 'What the hell's going on?' It was one of the few things he did for me. I said: 'Look, you know the problems with Kevin, he's got to go to your mother's.' Kevin jumped up and got hold of John. There was a bit of a struggle and eventually, John helped me calm Kevin down. John and I got Kevin into a cab and sent him home.

It was a horrendous night.

Some of my best decisions have been the quick ones where I haven't really had time to think. After I sent Kevin off home, I locked up and drove home for five o'clock. Halifax to Wakefield is not a long way but it takes thirty or forty minutes. A delivery was coming that morning so I had about an hour at home and then I went back to take the delivery after I had washed and showered again. When I got there, Kevin had rung and said he was coming down to see me. When he arrived, I said: 'Kevin, what are you trying to do to me? I'm sorry for what happened last night, we've got to deal with what's happened, but...'

Suddenly, before I could finish he apologised and then burst out crying. In that split second, I just said: 'There's the keys, I'll give you a call in a couple of days. Get on with it!' From then on, our relationship lasted another ten years – I don't think we ever had a problem after that, he responded to my trust. And it happened in a split second. As I was driving back to Halifax I was thinking, 'I'm going to kill that Kevin after what he put me through.' Determined to sack him and be done, I also felt sorry for the girl involved who was hurt (at that time we did not know she had died). When he started crying, I couldn't sack him. In an instant I changed my mind and made the decision to give him another chance. And I never regretted it; instant decisions are sometimes the best ones.

The nightclub had two entrances: one was on the pub side, and the other was the nightclub side. When people came in, they went upstairs to the nightclub room. In the middle, in a little alleyway, there was a fish and chip shop with a very small restaurant and outside sales as well in this narrow space. We decided to let the fish and chip shop to Stephen Quill, one of Kevin's brothers, and for quite a time there was no problem. Then a second brother, John, who had helped me calm Kevin down after the accident, rented it, which I soon learned was a big mistake. For a while he was running it quite happily and everything was OK, then one day I walked past the door and said cheerily: 'How are you doing? Is everything all right?'

I was shocked to see three Asian faces looking back at me. They were complete strangers and there was no sign of Kevin's brother John, who was supposed to be running the fish and chip shop. So I went back and looked in again. This time they looked back at me, bewildered. 'Excuse me, where's John?' I asked. One guy said: 'Ah, John no longer here. I bought fish and chip shop.' 'He doesn't even own the vinegar bottle, he was just renting it!' I told him. They couldn't believe it and said: 'How come, what do you mean?'

So I went to find Kevin and asked him if he had seen what was going on at the fish and chip shop. 'Where's your John?' I asked him. He said: 'I've no idea.' I explained that the new people had just turned up, thinking they had bought the business from John, who, of course, had no right to sell it. We ended up going to court over it and obviously the judge could see quite clearly what had happened. He told them: 'You're going to have to leave, you've got no right to be there. Somebody has sold you something that is not his to sell.' They weren't happy and demanded their money back. I said: 'That's your business. Don't look at me, I haven't had your money.'

Running a nightclub does plunge you into a different world. It's not quite the same now but at the time it seemed as if after 12 o'clock everything changes. Normal people who value their lives and their families and their jobs all go home because they need to be in bed. What's left is the funny, frequently difficult, side of society. Often it was the violent, the drunk or just the lonely or lively people who stayed out and hit the clubs. Midnight was the changeover time when it came to behaviour. Whenever anything happened, it was always after midnight, but bear in mind that back in those days the clubs used to close at two in the morning.

For some reason in Halifax, whether it was because of the relationship with the police or fear of 'them Quills', we never shut at two o'clock and always stayed open longer than anyone else. We used to get away with it because we had a top floor and everybody would go up there. In fact, we used to charge them to go up there. It was a scheme instigated by Kevin, not by me, but it certainly worked. We got an extra night out of it, and we probably got an extra couple of hours at night. Happily, it meant a lot of extra income. We weren't challenged by the police, so we kept it going. Looking back, I think it was nine years of purgatory, but at the time I didn't realise because I was earning a wage.

I used to stay until about one o'clock at least and then drive home. We had some good nights and some good weeks; they were different days. Nowadays, good business in clubs in town centres is generally confined to two days a week, Fridays and Saturdays. Even Fridays can be quiet, and really, only Saturdays are a big night. When we opened the Carousel it used to be busy from Wednesday right through to Sunday. It was a fantastic business and at that time I was earning a good wage. My friends were electricians, joiners, architects, who were all earning good money too. Flipping into clubs as well as shops, all of a sudden I found I could earn more money but my instinct wasn't just to earn more money so I could think,

'What can I buy?' – it was more, 'What can I buy next to improve our business?'

CHAPTER EIGHT

MECCA AND MORE

I loved the Carousel but about two years later, in 1984, I got the chance to buy the old Mecca in Manningham Lane, Bradford, which was much larger and had enormous potential. Someone had already bought it from Mecca and was running it as a nightclub called Caesar's at Tiffany's. The owner concerned, who was now looking to sell the place on, was a colourful character called Annis Abrahams. He exuded charisma, wore stylish salmon-coloured suits, had a bit of a suntan and looked a little like Aristotle Onassis. I was surprised to discover he was Welsh!

The potential was enormous, but so too was the price. Annis Abrahams wanted £390,000 for the freehold. However, there was a big car park on the side and I believed instantly that we could do great business there. The brewery was impressed with what I'd done with the Carousel, selling far more drink than the previous owner and increasing the barrelage to impressive proportions. They were more than happy to support me in this second venture. I offered £360,000. Annis Abrahams accepted, but he said pointedly: 'Where are you going to get your money?' I said: 'Well, I've got a letter from the brewery, saying for this particular premises they'll lend me £220,000.'

I explained that I had been to my own bank for the rest of the money. Unfortunately, by this time Mr Shackleton had left NatWest so I no longer had any personal contact. When I applied for a loan, they asked me what kind of business it was. I said it was a nightclub. I didn't think it would make any difference that it was not a shop, but the answer was firm and non-negotiable: 'We don't lend money for nightclubs.' So I faced losing this great opportunity because I could not borrow enough money. I knew I needed cash on top of the price to refurbish the place. I had £40,000, but I was still some £100,000 short.

So I told Annis Abrahams the situation. He was clearly keen to sell the place and he said: 'Will you meet me in Leeds tomorrow at 10 o'clock? I would like to introduce you to my bank.' I agreed to come along. His bank was the Allied Irish Bank and the next morning I found myself sitting in front of a manager I had never met, with no idea what Annis was going to say. In the event, he was very brief. He simply told the puzzled manager: 'I have got £7 million in your bank. Chris Edwards here wants to borrow £100,000. Lend him it or I will take my money out tomorrow.' Then he stood up and left the room.

I was stunned – I think I just said 'Wow!' – and the bank manager seemed a little taken aback as well. He said to me:

'You know I can't respond to that kind of talk, I'm running a bank here. Quite obviously, I can't lend you money on the basis of a threat.' But then he went on: 'What I am prepared to do is to come and see what you do. Show me what you do.'

By this time I'd got one nightclub in Halifax and three shops and I was living in a nice house. He wanted to see where I lived and everything I had. So I took him to see my house and to the nightclub; I took him to the three shops too. By then I also had a very limited warehousing facility and so I showed him that as well. As we were getting out of the car at the end of all that, he told me: 'I'm going to lend you the money.'

There were no plans or projections and not a spreadsheet in sight. I like to think he let me have the loan because he picked up on my energy, looked me in the eye and believed I was speaking with honest enthusiasm. I still bank there today with my personal banking and I've used them for business as well. On and off, over thirty years I've seen about six bank managers come and go, so when I pay them a visit they tend not to give me any trouble because they know I'm part of the furniture. I don't go in regularly, but I do know them all and when they start trying to give me a bit of lip or get a bit cheeky, I just say: 'Look, I've been here longer than any of you lot, thirty-two years I've been here! Where's my gold watch?'

When I borrowed the money I actually put my house, my dad's house and my brother's house against the loan; I wanted that club so badly. Dad and Laurie never hesitated to give me the backing that I wanted. At first I was fearless, then I woke up in the middle of the night, feeling absolutely terrified. 'If it all goes wrong, my whole family will be homeless,' I thought. It was quite a risk.

We opened up the nightclub in 1984 and for six years we never looked back. It was a massive undertaking. The place needed complete refurbishment and my budget was tight, to say the least. I had bought a 35,000 square foot nightclub and after I'd spent my £40,000, I had about £25,000 left to do a refurb! These days, you can't do one room for twenty-five grand, let alone a place with 35,000 square feet, and even then I had to spread my money pretty carefully. I got a few friends who were painters and decorators to help me out and we gave it a rough makeover.

We advertised the club under the new name of Dollars and it was very successful. Very quickly, we were pulling people from all over the place. We started getting celebrities in to do personal appearances. At the time Radio 1 DJs were very popular so we had them. We also had soap stars, especially ones from *EastEnders*, because it was massive at the time. In fact, we packed the place out, so much so that Annis Abrahams rang me every Sunday morning to ask me: 'What have you done this week?' When I told him what my attendances had been, his voice was very patronising as he said: 'Well done!'

Business-wise, it was another successful move and I had my family by my side too. When it comes to handling money there's no one you can trust more. My dad started doing the box office at Dollars and Mum was then doing the same job at the Carousel. During the nights, I was commuting between the two. Fortunately, it's not a great distance and it only took me about thirty minutes to travel between them.

* * * * *

As I have said, we had a lot of celebrities, especially stars who were doing concerts in the area. St George's Hall in Bradford was closed down for a while so a lot of their pre-booked concerts had nowhere else to go; we were approached and we staged them at Dollars. We did many concerts featuring acts like Terence Trent D'Arby, Little and Large and The Drifters. Around this time we started getting involved in the celebrity scene and so we booked stars from The Three Degrees to Roy 'Chubby' Brown for one-off appearances. We also staged a boxing match, an eliminator for a title fight. Life was certainly far from dull!

When Holly Johnson of Frankie Goes To Hollywood came to make a personal appearance, I had forgotten to tell my dad on the door who was coming. We had pre-booked Holly to come and given his agent a couple of hundred quid, as arranged. He didn't come to sing, just to be there and sign a few autographs. The agent arrived at the door, introduced Holly and explained that he was the lead singer of the high-flying pop group, Frankie Goes To Hollywood. Unimpressed, Dad told him flatly: 'I don't care *who* he is! If he doesn't pay £5, he doesn't come in.' The agent later told me that Dollars was the only place Holly had appeared where it had cost the two of them a tenner to get in! 'I couldn't believe it, but your dad was never going to budge,' he said.

I think Holly Johnson thought it was a bit of a laugh but Terence Trent D'Arby wasn't quite so easy-going. Apparently when he came to Dollars he had never sung to a live audience before. I don't know how we ended up booking him, but he was preparing to support Elton John on tour. We could hold around 2,000 people for a live show. Mr D'Arby wanted to rehearse for three or four nights. At the time we were between managers and I was managing the place myself. I used to let everyone in and then go to football training; I would go back and lock up afterwards. Terence Trent D'Arby was quite popular at the time and one of my best friends, Gary Dobson, the electrician who was centre half for our football team, said he wanted to come in and watch him. 'Yes, that's fine. They'll be finishing off rehearsing,' I said. Dollars had retained the massive dance floor of the old Mecca and Terence Trent D'Arby was rehearsing and singing onstage when Gary walked into the middle of this huge space and looked up at him. Suddenly, the singing stopped and one of Mr D'Arby's minders came up and said to Gary: 'Excuse me, would you move to one side? You're putting him off!'

Another big mistake we made was with the colourful comedian, Roy 'Chubby' Brown, who used to come to us twice a year for quite a few years. On one occasion we made a major blunder. Live entertainment at the nightclub always went on at 9.30pm. The doors opened at eight o'clock or even earlier as we let people enjoy a build-up to whatever acts were on. We had failed to advertise that Chubby was expecting to go onstage at his usual time of 8.30pm. One of the main reasons he liked to go on early was so that his crowd did not get drunk and start heckling him (no comedian likes hecklers).

We got to a point where he was ready to go on and we had pre-sold just short of 1,000 tickets and we'd only got 80 people in the club. That meant there were about another 900 still to come in so I had to go and see Chubby in his dressing room. I said to him: 'We've got nobody in yet, can you delay a little?' He looked at me and told me flatly: 'Chubby always goes on at 8.30.' I said: 'Look, you're going to have to give me another half an hour because we've made a bollocks of the timing. We never said what time we open but people will assume it's the time of normal opening time, which is 9.30.' So when half an hour had passed, I went back to him and we still had only half of the ticket holders in and so I had to persuade him to delay again. He told me: 'I'm going to give you another 30 minutes because if I get hecklers, I can't do me job.' Another half an hour went by and we had another couple of hundred people in, but we were still a long way from being full. I knew he wasn't going to budge any more so I went to the DJ, who was doing the announcing, and said: 'Make it the longest introduction you've ever done.'

I went round to placate the star but Chubby is no fool – he's been a hugely popular comic for donkey's years. So I was talking to him and he said: 'Is he going to announce me or not?' 'He's a bit long-winded, he'll get round to it,' I told him. We managed to waste another fifteen minutes or so and a few more ticket holders arrived. Chubby eventually went on, but he smiled at me later and said: 'You bastard!' But he went on, and it went all right – we had about 90 per cent of the crowd in by the time he went onstage.

Not all the stars were so hard to handle. We booked The Three Degrees and that was taking a massive risk. Remember, this was in the 1980s, when they were the favourite group of Prince Charles, and they were very expensive. Happily, it turned out they were very nice people and I can recall some magical moments as my two daughters, Sonya and Nicola, who would only have been three and six at the time, ended up singing and dancing with The Three Degrees when they were onstage rehearsing.

* * * * *

Nightclubs are an extremely competitive business and like any owner, I would always try my utmost to attract customers. A favourite ruse was to try and get a famous face to put in a well-publicised appearance at the Carousel on the way to my bigger venue of Dollars. At the time the biggest soap character on British television was 'Dirty Den' Watts, the ruthless love cheat played in *EastEnders* by actor Leslie Grantham. He was right at the top of his game when I picked him up at Leeds Bradford Airport and tried my usual line in persuasion.

In those days I would go and pick the stars up personally and take them to what they thought was the venue. I used to book them for just the one visit to one of our venues and would then try to squeeze in another appearance from them for free! Otherwise I'd face a double payment. I was always very polite, because I *am* polite, and when we were driving, I'd say: 'Look, would you do me a massive favour, please? I've got a very small pub in Halifax, it's only five minutes down the road (although it was at least half an hour), would you stick your face in there and surprise all the regulars?' It was a gamble because by then I had already advertised their visit at both places! They nearly always agreed. In fact, I can't remember anyone saying no. It helped me a lot because two visits would have cost me much more and we were running on a very tight budget.

Leslie Grantham seemed like a proper down-to-earth bloke and he said: 'Yeah, I'll do that for you.' I got him in the car – I had a two-seater sports car. The journey started to drag a little and he said: 'I thought you said it was five minutes.' 'It's only just round the corner,' I said, as cheerfully as I could. And when we drove round the corner, in anticipation that he would agree to the stunt, we had done press releases and everything else. So when we arrived in Halifax town centre you could hear this big buzz of noise building up. All the women were shouting: 'We want Den!' He turned to me and said: 'Have I been tricked?' There was a crowd outside the club because not everyone could get in; he was so popular. I wound the window down to try and get people to move out of the way and a woman came up to the side and she said: 'Where's Den?' 'He's here!' I said. 'I'll kiss you, you're good enough,' she told me, and she gave me a kiss on the cheek. And I was only sitting next to him!

We got in, and unbeknown to me, Kevin had alerted the *Daily Mirror* in advance so we got in the newspapers as well. We had organised a woman to welcome Den and she whipped off her top and that went straight in the *Mirror* – 'Housewife Strips For Den' was the headline. The things you do to get free publicity! Leslie did all that for free and eventually I got him back in the car. I took him back to Dollars, which was equally busy, and it went really well. He just laughed off the extra appearance and said I was a 'cheeky bastard', which I suppose I was on that occasion. He was a good man. At the time it was a great coup because everyone wanted Dirty Den. I think the stars were sympathetic when they realised this was my business and not just part of some great anonymous corporate group. Not one of them let me down, they all did both venues. Then later on we had Anita Dobson, who played Dirty Den's long-suffering wife Angie, and she was a very nice woman.

The comedian Duncan Norvelle was a little different. We staged a round of the Miss UK contest at Dollars in Bradford in 1985 but we really didn't get a choice; it was supposed to be somewhere else and at the last minute they asked us if we would do it. A girl from Bradford called Mandy Shires won and she went on to become Miss UK and a runner up in Miss World. The qualification round happened to be the night when we had Duncan Norvelle booked, so I rang him and told him the beauty contest was on and I asked if he would support us and help out as compère. He agreed, but on the night there was a bit of a problem with the sound system. We had to alter everything and he was getting feedback and he was getting very, very annoyed with it. We thought we could get over it and so Duncan went into the back to get changed. There were some pictures in his dressing room that he took a fancy to, even though they were pretty ordinary. He said: 'I like these pictures, can I have them?' 'Yes, you're doing me a favour. You can have the pictures,' I told him. So he took them all down and put them in his car. Later, we couldn't get over the sound system problems well enough to satisfy him, so he stormed out, got into his car and drove off... with our paintings and without doing the show! Needless to say, we'd only paid a deposit. I wouldn't pay him the balance until afterwards anyhow and I couldn't pay him in this case because he was gone. After what happened, I certainly didn't feel like paying him the rest. The next day, his agent rang me and when I explained what had happened, he said: 'Forget the balance, we'll call it a draw.'

* * * * *

Of course it's not all light-hearted showbiz fun running a club. Sometimes there is a need to have a little bit of strength on your side. I used to have a doorman called Tom. He looked like one of the Kray brothers and his attitude was often not unlike theirs. Whoever paid him his wages became his best friend, so he became a good friend of mine. Dollars had two parts to it: there was the big nightclub and then there was a little disco area, which the old Mecca used to call 'Bali Eye'. After a while we decided to refurbish the little bar and because we had renamed the place Dollars, we called it Dimes so it was Dollars and Dimes. A bit corny perhaps, but it worked. We replaced the carpet and at the end we had some spare carpet left over. I always like to look after the pennies and I thought maybe it would come in handy if any carpet was damaged in the future but then this leftover carpet mysteriously disappeared.

I later found out from Tom that he had just been in the pub down the road and seen my carpet neatly fitted in the bar! Tom always worked on commission with me. 'How much was that carpet worth?' he asked. 'Something like £1,500,' I told him. We realised it must have been our builder who had taken the carpet for a quick resale. Tom said: 'We should be getting that money from them.' So we got the builder in and sat him down on one side of my desk, with Tom and me on the other. I challenged him that he had fitted my carpet into the pub. He said: 'Well, I thought it was surplus.' 'No, it's not surplus. I was going to keep it for fill-ins for if we have any damage,' I told him. He asked what it was worth and I told him £1,500, looking at the square footage. 'Well, I'll pay you for it then,' he offered. I said: 'Well, if you pay me, you're only putting me back where I was. I had £1,500 worth of carpet and all you're going to do is pay me for something you were prepared to steal. So you were going to steal it and I would lose £1,500 and I wasn't supposed to know. Now I want £1,500 for the carpet and £1,500 profit that you were going to pinch off me.'

Tom was growling away next to me, so the builder paid me £3,000.

* * * * *

It was important to have my parents involved in my businesses because they were obviously the people I trusted most in the world. Everything I've ever done has been a family affair, but there were times when you didn't want your own mother too close to the action! As the years went on, Thursday nights were sometimes a problem when it came to generating business for Dollars. We became desperate and started putting on all sorts of entertainment on. By the back end of the 1980s, we had groups like Marmalade and loads of others, but that didn't always work and we were keen to have different acts, so we decided to put on a lady who did a risqué act involving a snake.

I don't think we really knew 100 per cent that she was a stripper, but we hoped she would bring in a good audience. It was unfortunate for me that it was one of the nights when my dad was on the door and Mum wasn't needed at Halifax, so she was there as well. She came to Dollars and she was looking over the balcony when the lady came on with her snake and removed all doubt about whether or not she was a stripper, along with most of her clothes! By all accounts she was going down very well, until my mother intervened. I don't think the snake offended her, but she certainly was offended by the stripping. I wasn't there at the time. Mum freaked out and made Simon James the DJ turn all the lights out and put a sudden end to the performance. She said: 'My son can't have known this was going on.' Of course I did know but I never admitted it. Anyway, she had it all turned off. I think our area manager Ken Delecki was there at the time. He took her to one side and he and Simon calmed her down. Eventually the show went on. It had to go on because people had paid to watch it, but my mother was very offended.

* * * * *

Because Dollars was in Bradford, a city where racial issues were often to the fore at that time, we never wanted to be prejudiced against any race. When we were really busy, we would have ten doormen: three Asian, three West Indian and four white English guys. On a busy Saturday we would get 1,800 people in from all sorts of races – it was a big club.

Someone I would later have been quite happy *not* to let in was a particular Radio 1 personality, one of many DJs who came. When they got to know us, they would often call in. Typically, this particular DJ would ring on his way back from a gig somewhere in the north and say: 'Do you want me to come in and do an appearance?' In those days, in clubs, it was always a bit of a coup if you could get a famous face to arrive. All he had to do was get up, say a few words and play a few tunes. We'd give him a couple of hundred quid, our customers enjoyed the surprise and everyone was happy. Before one unadvertised visit, he said to me: 'Give me a couple of hundred quid and a case of wine.' I agreed. So he came and he did his thing and it was great. He said thanks, and he left. Next morning, the agent we normally used to book all these people rang me and we chatted about the weekend. I mentioned that the DJ had turned up. He seemed surprised and said: 'Why would he turn up?' Innocently, I said: 'Well, he just said, "Give me a case of wine and a couple of hundred quid and I'll do it."' I never thought about it at the time but I suppose the agent would have been concerned about his percentage and the fact that the DJ was taking business from him.

The next call I received was from the DJ himself. He started swearing down the phone at me, calling me a bastard and saying I should have had 'more f****ing sense' than to tell the agent he was normally booked through about the visit. Thinking about it afterwards, he was 100 per cent right and I was wrong. I should never have mentioned it so I perhaps deserved the right bollocking I got from him!

* * * * *

Dollars led me on to buying a pub that I decided to rename Fat Sam's. Previously known as the Midland Hotel, it was in the town centre of Pontefract. It was just a pub, which I was interested in because there was a nearby nightclub called Kikos up for sale. In those days you often used to have what they called a 'feeder bar'. Typically, this would be a pub in the middle of the town where nightclub customers could gather earlier in the evening. In this case the club was probably a ten-minute walk away. It seemed promising and so I bought the pub, thinking I would then do the deal on Kikos. The club should have followed, but unfortunately, someone outbid me.

I didn't have enough money to get it and so I ended up with just a very small pub in the middle of town.

We did a little work on the place and Fat Sam's got going. It was OK, although the chief claim to fame was that to liven up quiet Thursday nights I decided to introduce topless barmaids to the middle of Pontefract! It was a good idea that lasted three or four years until the standard of barmaid started to deteriorate and to put it bluntly, the things that the lads came in to see were not so pert anymore.

When it was busy, it was *really* busy. You're never quite sure where the audience is going to come from and how many will arrive, when you're planning to do a night. Pontefract is just off the M62 and when all the lorry drivers started taking an interest in our particular attraction we nearly bottle-necked Pontefract with lorries parked all over the place! They loved to call in and see the topless barmaids in Fat Sam's. It really did work; it was really good. I don't think we ever told my mum about it and fortunately, Pontefract was not somewhere she used to visit.

There were lots of incidents in Fat Sam's. I had that pub for eighteen to twenty years and it became a big part of my life. In the early days I used to make up the wages in the office on Friday nights and I would physically deliver the cash in packets. I would park in the same place every time on a yellow line, but because I used to turn up at 10.30 at night, I parked there for years and never had a problem. Then one day I came back to my car and there was a ticket on it. After such a long time I was shocked but never thought much about it and so I just paid the fine. The next week, I came back again and got another ticket. About six or eight weeks went by without further incident, but then it happened a third time. I came out to my car and the copper was there. I remembered the number of the copper so I knew it was the same policeman who had given me each ticket. I said: 'Why do you keep giving me tickets? I've been parking here forever and there is only you who ever gives me a ticket.' Realising he must have had some sort of grudge against me, I said: 'Why in all these years has no other police officer ever given me parking tickets? You are the only one.'

He was writing the ticket out and he held it up and then, just as he was giving it to me, I snatched it out of his hand. I didn't snatch it to stop him writing it, he had already finished – I wouldn't be daft enough to confront a copper in that way. When I snatched it, he grabbed me and he attracted the attention of two other bobbies near their 'meatwagon', which they used to throw people into. So they came over, handcuffed me and chucked me in the back of the van. They took me to the police station and because it was a Friday night in Pontefract – a lively place, to say the least – they actually put me in a holding cell while they were waiting to take my details.

I still had the wages for my staff at two nightclubs to deliver, but they didn't search me and they didn't take my phone from me. So I was in there, making calls to explain why I'd been delayed. I said that I didn't know what was happening but I'd be there as soon as I could; I asked the staff to hang on for their wages and promised I would be there eventually. A copper came in and asked: 'What are you doing, using your phone?' 'I've got responsibilities,' I said. I apologised but tried to explain no one had told me I couldn't use my phone. The copper I had clashed with was at the other end of the counter when they were questioning me. I said: 'Is his number on the ticket? That's the only thing I need to know.' They took the rest of my details, eventually let me go, and so I went back and paid the wages. Next morning, I was so annoyed, I rang Pontefract police station and asked to speak to the duty sergeant. I was put through to a duty inspector and after explaining who I was and what had been happening, I said, 'This is what I've done for the last fifteen years.'

The Inspector asked if I would come and see him. 'Do you want to press charges?' he said. I asked if he would be offended if I did so and he told me: 'No, I would probably encourage you' – because they had had problems with this particular bobby before. I said: 'I am annoyed. It's a bit embarrassing in my position to be bundled into the back of a van when all I did was snatch a ticket when he's the only person who's ever given me one.'

Anyway, we eventually found our way into court with this bobby and his evidence was all over the place; my solicitor found out that he had even made a call to the records department to check me out. My solicitor said: 'So we're in the middle of Pontefract and we've got a legitimate businessman, who has no record whatsoever. What would prompt you, unless you had a vendetta against him, to make that important call as all he's done is park his car on a yellow line? Was it personal?' I was awarded £1,500 from public funds and last time I heard, he was no longer in the force. So you get back at the end of the night and your wife asks, 'Have you had a good night?' You just smile and say: 'Fantastic!'

I'd been disappointed not to get Kikos because I knew it

was a club with real potential. Happily for me, the guy who bought it barely had it for twelve months before he got into financial difficulties. The brewery contacted me – the same brewery I used for Dollars and Halifax and Fat Sam's, and everything – they rang and said, 'If you are prepared to take on his debt, you can have the keys,' so that's what I did. I took on Kikos and Fat Sam's was then very successful as a feeder bar, as I had intended, and I ran that for twenty years.

* * * * *

It was when my nightclub business was in a bit of a lull that I met Louise, the girl who has been my partner in life for a long time now. Although Lorraine and I parted, we have stayed friends, especially because the children are very important to both of us. I made it clear to her that if I prospered financially then she would too. I also told her: 'If I end up skint, you'll be in the same boat!' That was more than twenty years ago, and I have kept my word: what I say is what I do.

I met Louise in a nightclub and she has worked very hard to keep the nightclub side of my business thriving ever since. When we first met she was working with some mutual friends who owned and ran the Rooftop Gardens in Wakefield. She was their personal assistant and played a very important role in their business.

When we met, Dollars and Halifax had gone and I just had Kikos and Fat Sam's. I was actually thinking of coming out of the nightclub business altogether, but Louise helped to change my mind and give me back my drive and enthusiasm. She eventually left her job and helped me build up the nightclub side of my business. We decided to consolidate what we had, which was the two in Pontefract. Then, working together, we opened two nightclubs in Bradford, four in Leeds and one in Manchester. Louise was instrumental in all that.

* * * * *

In my experience the life of a nightclub and bargain shop owner is never dull. By this time I had a BMW 7 series car and I used to park it at the back of Kikos, near the fire doors. It was a very handy spot – you just went up some stairs and you were in. One night, there was a bit of trouble in the club, which spilled outside. All the crates full of empty bottles were outside the back doors and some lads started throwing bottles at each other and every one that didn't hit somebody hit my car instead. All dented and damaged, it looked as if it had been in a stock-car race. But I was busy, and so it was left like that for quite a while. I could be seen driving round the streets of Wakefield in this new, but very battered BMW. One day, I got a call from the guy at the BMW garage, who knew me as a customer. 'Chris, what's happened to your car?' he asked me. I explained that I'd had a bit of a problem. He said: 'It's not good PR for us, will you please come in and let us sort it out?' They promised to do me a good deal, but they weren't quite upset enough to do it for free!

Another odd motoring incident occurred in Kikos in 1990 after I had parked just outside the front door on the main road. One of our doormen came to me and said: 'Who's in your car?' 'I've no idea, I came by myself!' I said. He insisted there was someone sitting in my car so I went outside and he was right. I opened the car door, and it was early evening and a lady was sitting inside with her shopping. 'Can I help you?' I said. She asked: 'Can you take me to Knottingley?' She thought I was a bloody taxi!

All the doormen were killing themselves laughing.

* * * * *

One night I had left and our female manager rang me because there had been a confrontation with the doormen about some long-forgotten grievance. She said: 'I'm here with a thousand people and the doormen have all walked out. The customers are helping themselves to the bar.' I told her: 'I'll turn round and come back.' But she was concerned because she thought I might be physically abused. When I got back, Dave Downes, the head doorman, had come over to find out what was going on and I just said: 'Dave, what the bloody hell are you doing to me?'

Pontefract is a small community, like Castleford or Barnsley, so the locals all knew our doormen had walked out and they must have thought, 'Let's go and help ourselves to the booze.' And that's just what they were doing. Dave was head of the nightclub doormen's company and he said: 'I think there's been a misunderstanding.' So he quickly got all the doormen back in and settled the situation down again. It probably cost me a couple of grand's worth of booze that people had grabbed before everything was under control!

Kevin Quill had left me quite a few years before and had ended up buying a couple of pubs and then he started a club in Leeds called the Fruit Cupboard. Some time before Christmas in 1996 he rang me out of the blue and told me all about it. I was pleased he was successful. He said the Fruit Cupboard was doing well, but he wanted to sell it because he was keen to move to Thailand. After closing Dollars some years earlier, we went back to Bradford and we had just opened another club called The Mirage.

Kevin asked me if I wanted to buy the Fruit Cupboard from him. The club was leasehold but he wanted to sell me the business operation. I went over, liked what I saw, and we agreed a price. There were other people looking at it, but he said he would rather sell it to me because of our relationship from years before and so I bought it.

It was a different sort of club back in the days before Leeds became much busier at nights. We used to have two very different busy nights: Friday was 'Frisco Disco', with a fully white crowd and popular eighties music, while Saturday was known as 'Sugar Daddys', which was R&B music and attracted more black, Asian and African people. It was quite a contrast. We would get customers who had a great night out on either Friday or Saturday. Then they would go back to the club on the alternative night, expecting it to be the same and the shock to the system was considerable. Instead of explaining it in advance, the doormen used to enjoy taking the money off people, letting them go in and then they would count the seconds away before they came rushing back out the door in shock. We used to have a lot of awkward moments, but in its day, it was a fantastic club.

That was going reasonably well, and so I moved on to establish another nightclub called Space in September 1999, which was also in Leeds. It proved to be one of the best moves I've ever made. That was sixteen years ago and I've still got it to this day. We entered into negotiations, but it needed a full re-fit. Then a television company rang and said they wanted to do a fly-on-the-wall documentary of building a nightclub. They were keen to follow the project right up to opening day. I could see the benefits of some free advertising, so I agreed. It was a really interesting operation because it was a major build: we had a lot of walls to move and a lot of RSJs to put in, because we were in the basement and there was a four-storey building above us. We got all the necessary work done and when we opened, because we had been on TV, people knew all about it and wanted to come and see for themselves.

While we were building the club, the television cameras kept coming in and recording. I refused to make an appearance because I just wasn't that kind of person at that time. There was a chirpy plasterer the TV people always interviewed and he became the star of the series. Very happy-go-lucky, he wore shorts, made jokes and hung in some strange positions to get his plastering done. Obviously, the TV people saw him as someone who could become a celebrity. On opening night, unfortunately for them, very quickly he went from extrovert to introvert. In his normal clothes he seemed extremely shy and limited, not at all like the joker viewers had seen in the earlier programmes. Intimidated away from his work mode, he'd gone from being incredibly hyper to being unable to put two words together. But for us the programmes worked wonders and Space was instantly popular.

Today, the Birdcage in Manchester, which opened in November 2006, is a thriving nightclub, with a richly deserved reputation for top-quality flamboyant shows and colourful drag queens. It is impressive, but the Birdcage in Leeds, which opened in November 2001, came first and it really was quite something. It was another idea I had had in my head for quite a few years. I took a trip to Blackpool and visited a club called Funny Girls, which was really just a bar with drag queens. I'm not quite sure why I went because as a young man I was never interested in the gay scene. But as you get older, you start to realise that everything in life is not so black and white. There are always great characters and decent people in every walk of life. I've met some wonderful and genuine people who are gay and they became good friends.

After I had visited Funny Girls, I was impressed by the glamour and the humour of it all and so I thought, 'I can do this, but I don't want to do it in a pub. I want to do it in a nightclub.' So I tried a couple of venues but failed to get them. Then our property agent, Mike Francis, who helped me to get Space and who also works with us finding shop premises, rang me out of the blue. He said: 'There's a basement where I think you can get a licence just round the corner from where Space was, just down the road.' So I had a look and I thought, 'That'll do for my Birdcage.' To be honest, I didn't have the name then – I didn't know what to call it. In my head it was just my nightclub-cum-drag venue.

We did the deal with Landsec, a major property company. I lease shops from them as well, so we already had a relationship and that helped. We built the club for £700,000, which was more borrowed money. I don't believe you can get such value for money now; it was a big risk. We were situated opposite Yates' Wine Lodge so we were a little bit on the circuit. While building it up, I realised my big problem was that I didn't have any drag queens and I had no idea how to find them.

Without Louise I would never have managed it. In the end we cobbled together some auditions and started searching. First, we just wanted DJs and so we found a couple of old-fashioned guys who could certainly talk and on the first opening night these two DJs were very chatty and all that. That night was a great success but I knew it wasn't what I wanted; we had the perfect venue but we didn't have the perfect entertainment. I said firmly: 'We'll have to use them this weekend but it's not what I want.' The next night I learned that a drag DJ called Miss Orry had applied and wanted to do an audition so we arranged to bring him in early evening before opening on the Friday. We were in the club and all of a sudden, he picked the mic up. I was pottering away doing something and you know when you think, 'That's it' – and that *was* it. He had plenty of confidence and some good jokes so I agreed to pay him a lot of money and gave him a job. We soon packed the place out just on the back of him being a good draw; he was just a compère with a wicked sense of humour. He was great and his signing led to a very successful seven or eight years.

Right from the start he approached me and said: 'Do you want me to do a drag show for you? It's all right, me being on my own, but I can only go through my jokes a few times before they become very repetitive because I haven't got a big repertoire. I can't keep changing it.' So we built a six-person show with two drag queens, two girl dancers and two male dancers. Then we did shows, which were basically copies of big musicals like *Cabaret* and *Dream Girls*. With every record there is a video, so what we were doing was copying the video but with drag queens. That was the predecessor of Manchester, which started later. At one time we had the Birdcage, Leeds and the Birdcage, Manchester operating successfully at the same time. Quite quickly, the Leeds version became popular.

We were packed inside and for years we had people queuing round the block each night. Because of the location it was very expensive to run and it was like a destination venue – good for Fridays and Saturdays for entertainment, but not much use on other nights. Still, it soon became a special place, everyone's choice for party and event nights. Midweek, we concentrated more on drinks promotions.

Success sometimes breeds problems. For ten years we opened five nights a week. To get people in on the less popular nights – Wednesday, Thursday, Sunday – we used to have drinks promotions. Unfortunately, what often comes with these promotions is a little bit of trouble. We could keep a lid on the internal trouble, but at one point the police challenged our licences. For a time I felt they were unfairly against me. On some occasions they seemed to take things beyond what appeared to me to be the call of duty: we had to go to legal reviews to defend the licences and it began to cost me a great deal of money. We actually went to a judicial review in London.

The opposition was very, very expensive and difficult to deal with, and then there was a change of hierarchy in the police. I went to a meeting with the police and spelt out my side of the story, explaining how I thought we had been victimised. The police never agreed we had been victimised but within twenty-four hours the pressure was off. It had cost us more than £100,000 to defend ourselves from unfair accusations. During the problems I had had a confrontation with the senior police officer concerned. It happened after we both found our way to the wrong magistrates' court by mistake. By chance, we happened to be standing next to each other and he said:

'Can I ask you something? Do you earn as much money out of your nightclubs as you do out of your shops?'

I couldn't believe what I was hearing and so I said to him: 'What makes you think I earn any money at all? I just work hard!' That encounter gave me a flavour of the sort of person he was. Perhaps he was motivated by jealousy, I don't know, but I still don't feel it was an appropriate question for him to ask. Normally, I just stay happy, I don't gloat, I don't show off and I don't think I've ever got enough money because my overheads are always more than the money I've got. If I don't earn, I'm out of business. I'm happy to say that for years now we have had a good relationship with the police. The vast majority of the officers I have encountered have been fair and honourable. They have a very difficult job to do and we are always keen to be as helpful as possible.

* * * * *

The Leeds Birdcage was always close to my heart. It was a highly successful club that gave me a lot of satisfaction over ten years and it ended strangely, yet very happily, for me as well. The finish came after the landlords approached us and said: 'Look, there's a new big shopping centre called Trinity, which is going to be the next enormous development in Leeds.' The Birdcage was right underneath the new centre. The landlords said: 'You can stay open as you are long leaseholders because we're not going to touch your property, but we are going to have to give you a temporary entrance.' By this time the business, though still profitable, was not as good as it had been. I said: 'I can't run with a temporary entrance. Nightclubs don't work like that, we need to be big and bold and easily accessible. Our customers will be put off by a temporary entrance.' We negotiated an agreement in which they paid me so much to close while all the construction work went on above, leaving us to mothball the whole place. Then they would give me more money in eighteen months' time to help promote the reopening. To me that sounded like a great deal – I could have eighteen months rest from it all and get my energy together again.

But that summer, about two or three years ago, it simply never stopped raining. The whole time, the big new Trinity development was open to the weather throughout. It kept on raining and the developers hadn't got a cover on it. I don't know where they thought the rain was finding its way to, but I soon found out: it was in the Birdcage. We'd given them the keys and mothballed everything. We'd agreed that we could go in once a month just to make sure everything was OK because obviously we had an expensive computer set-up for the show as all the lights were synchronised with the music in this system. Called Showmagic, it was programmed so all the musical timing was in sync with the screens. It was very professional, as Manchester Birdcage is to this day. Then one month when we turned up to take a look the developers said: 'No, you can't come in. We've had a bit of a problem.' The 'bit of a problem' was that the place was under six feet of water! So that brought us into another discussion.

They said: 'Don't worry, we're going to get rid of the water. We're going to dry it all out.' But I wasn't happy. I said: 'You can't dry it out to my satisfaction, this is a major refurb.' After many negotiations, which were helped by the good relationship we had with Landsec, eventually we negotiated a settlement. I just never re-opened it, gave them the keys back and they paid me a sum to close it, which was substantially more than I'd paid to open it. They had paid me £300,000 in compensation for closing down for all the work to be done and then, when there was no way back for the Birdcage, they gave me two chunks of money, which added up to £980,000 to walk away! The Birdcage in Leeds was a brilliant experience. I had it for about ten years – the first six were was fantastic, while the next four were OK.

The generous payout was good news but there was some very bad news that immediately followed it. At the same time we were having a legal problem over a nightclub called Mashed in Bradford, one of the last places I opened. It traded all right, but then the old town centre moved and we started to struggle with it. Unfortunately, Mashed ended up in a major legal issue, which was very expensive. Basically, I received over £1 million for the Birdcage exit, while getting out of Mashed ended up costing me £1.1 million. In a nutshell, one compensated for the other, but at least I got out.

* * * * *

In Leeds, some years ago, there were big problems with something I never took part in, and never condoned: drugs. For a while they were rife there. We took a very firm line and did our best to keep both drug dealing and drug taking away from our clubs. I think the police realised we were taking a firm stance but some of the drug dealers were characters and it was not good business to make enemies of these people. My attitude was that we didn't attack drugs but we didn't condone them either. If we saw some drug dealing in one of our clubs, we would take them off you, and put you out.

Among our many colourful customers there was one character I really liked. Known as Mad Dog John, he was just one of the many unusual people that you come up against in the nightclub world. Now, you don't get a nickname like that from regular attendance at Sunday school! He wasn't mad – in fact, he was a very sensible lad, who was extremely smart as well as being very tall. He used to come in, and he had a reputation about him. Always, he was very courteous to me, though. By then I was of an age when he knew I didn't want anything to do with drugs. I made it clear to him that he didn't sell drugs in our club and I'm not sure if he did, or he didn't. He asked to book Space for his thirtieth birthday; he wanted a private party. I asked the doorman and he said that John was all right and wouldn't cause any problems. We had a really good night for his party and I chatted to him quite a lot. Normally, I would keep people like him at arm's-length and didn't drink with them or become too friendly with them. I never let people, including John, buy me a drink and would make sure that I bought the drink myself. But I liked him. He had a bit of a reputation and he was going in one of our clubs, but I had told the head doorman that John could come in because he wasn't causing us any problems.

Then I got a message saying he had been banned because he had punched the DJ in Rehab, another Leeds club I had by then taken over. It was out of the blue and I was surprised. The message was passed on to Space and we just thought, 'If he's going to behave like that, we don't want him in our clubs.' Then a few days later I got a call from John himself. He said: 'Chris, they're barring me from your clubs.' 'What have you been doing, John?' I responded. He asked me to let him come back in. I thought I needed to meet him and sort things out, so I said: 'I need to talk to you.' So I met him at Tiger, Tiger in Leeds to keep him away from our places. We sat down, I got him a beer, and I said: 'John, you know the situation. You're a businessman yourself.' What you find with these people is that if they respect you and you give them respect, then they will do anything for you. I don't mean financially, but they'll look out for you, watch your back for you, so it always pays to stay friends. But this particular lad I liked because he was a genuine sort. I said: 'John, you know I can't overrule my security staff and let you in.'

By this time I had four clubs in Leeds: the Birdcage, Space, Fruit Cupboard and Rehab. So I rang the Birdcage up and cleared John to go in there. I said to him: 'I've spoken to Ricky, who is the head doorman of the Birdcage. I know it's not your kind of venue but you can go in there any time. He's happy for you to go in but the other three, do me a favour, leave it a couple of months, then ring me again and I promise you if nothing has gone wrong, I'll get them to let you in.' Because I'd given him time and listened to him he shook my hand and I thought, 'Well, he'll be all right for two months.'

The following Saturday, I heard the shocking news that he had been shot dead! So I never got the chance to find out whether or not my way of dealing with John was going to work. I saw him on the Thursday and he got shot on the Saturday. But it didn't frighten me – the whole club world brings you into association with some colourful characters.

* * * * *

I don't know Peter Stringfellow. He's not somebody I have ever really spoken to, but I do admire what he's done. I read his book and I thought it was a fantastic story. In the early days, he used to get his mother to do the door of one of his nightclubs and for many years I used both my parents on the box offices of my clubs. I loved having them involved and as I have already said, there's nothing quite like having someone you can really trust when it comes to handling money.

In his heyday Peter Stringfellow became very, very famous and he is quite a character. But that has never been my way; I've done a lot with clubs without ever being the face of the club. I've always ducked out of the publicity. To me, it's just a business – I've not got that sort of ego.

* * * * *

Dishonesty and drugs were the two challenges of life in the nightclub business but Leeds, a decade or so ago, was like lots of other cities. Many young people had gone off drink and started 'doing' drugs. I myself have never done drugs and I don't understand them: I always want to be in a position where if someone was to put a lie detector on me, I could insist I've never taken drugs and pass the test. Apart from Mad Dog John, there were one or two characters going round Leeds who were known to be involved with drugs. I don't know if they were the actual dealers or working for someone else, but there were some high-profile characters. One guy who comes to mind is an African lad they used to call Reds. He had gold teeth and was a very friendly, likeable person, but almost certainly up to no good!

Reds was one of many I got to know. Like Mad Dog, they

were the guys you would keep at arm's-length and not get too involved with. What we didn't realise at the time was that there was a big Leeds police undercover operation going on against drugs. They were placing officers in the community tasked to find out the main dealers. You don't realise these sort of operations go on, but this one certainly took place. Whoever was undercover in our place would have given us a whiter-than-white rating, though, because we had a zero tolerance policy towards drugs.

But they weren't just investigating the venues; they were looking for the leading lights of the drugs trade too. They wanted to know who was doing the dealing. One of the undercover coppers had befriended this guy Reds, so he found out lots of information. I believe five or six major dealers were scooped up and arrested in one weekend.

The dealers were all characters; you just kept away from their nasty sides. I never asked about the drugs because I didn't want to know but the Leeds police did a fantastic job the weekend of the drugs operation. Space at that time was a very popular club; it was the place the footballers used to come to. Now, all these years later, we are still busy but it's a bit different now, with student nights Tuesdays, Wednesdays, all through the week. Space is now a student club but from my point of view, it's still a very decent venue.

* * * * *

In any cash business there is always theft. One of my worst experiences was with a particular manager, who I will not name. He was doing a pretty good job. I respected him because he'd been there for a while but he had a strange habit of frequently bringing his 'rich dad' into the conversation for no apparent reason. One day, he turned up in a sports car. It was not that expensive, but it was a nice flashy car and evidently a gift. Then, another day, he turned up on an expensive motorbike that caught my eye. 'Yes, my dad's bought it for me,' he said. He used to tell us that his dad was giving him and his brother some money. Of course I should have known then that something wasn't quite right, but because he was doing a good job, I let it go. I knew where he lived, and I just didn't see the danger signals at that point. It seemed quite feasible that the tales of his generous dad were true.

Out of the blue one day he said to me that if I ever wanted to sell a certain pub he would be very interested in buying it. He indicated that his father would be providing the funds and that he thought he might even be able to run it separately, as well as doing his job with me. I never thought that much about that either.

Very soon afterwards the assistant manager rang up and said: 'I think we might have a problem.' I went straight over to see him. We had just had a Bank Holiday Sunday, which was normally very busy in this particular club. The assistant said that, unusually, the manager in question had told him he could leave a little bit early. Before he left, he had noted we were having a fantastic night so he looked on the screen in the office to see how much we had taken; he thought we were going to break a record for how busy we were on the bar. When he saw the figure he thought it was high, but when he got back in on the Monday to cash up, it was a little lower. He showed me everything and we both came to the same conclusion: the manager was fiddling.

The employee in question had booked to go on holiday about a week or a fortnight later. We wondered how he was deducting the money. The system was all computerised and we couldn't work out how he was managing it. We rang the till people who did all the software and asked if there was anything they knew about their system that might explain what he was up to. They said yes, there was a back system they could get into, which would tell them the true figures. We decided to have a free run and get all the evidence together while our suspect was on holiday; we just played it along, but while we were playing it along for that week, I went back to him. Just to test him, I said: 'I've been thinking about selling the pub and I'm a bit short of money at the moment. If you can do me a quick deal, I'll do it on the cheap for you.' It was probably valued at £300,000 at the time so I told him that I would let him have it for £200,000, but I needed a £20,000 deposit so he gave me £20,000. He should never have had £20,000; that was obvious to me. So he went off on his holidays, we got the computer people in and they ran it right back as far as it would go. Of course there was a limit to how far that was, but they could go back to almost when the manager started. I forget the actual sum he had stolen from me, but I think it was in excess of £100,000!

He had been bringing a dozen bottles of vodka in and taking the money he took for them at nightclub prices out of the system. Now we had all the evidence we needed. Perhaps we sometimes underestimate the police but our man got back home on his flight at midnight, kids in tow, and the police were there at six o'clock in the morning. We thought he was quite a tough, strong-willed character, but the police said as soon as they picked him up, he sang like a canary. He admitted everything and put up no smokescreen or excuses. In fact, he said to me it had actually got to the point where, because he was bringing his booze in and just selling it, he thought that was all right. The outcome was that he was going to have to go to court. He rang me and said: 'Chris, can you tell me what the hell's going on? This is doing my wife's head in.' I just said: 'What do you expect me to do? I'll see you in court.' He was going to do time because it was systematic stealing, but the police said: 'Do you want him in court, or do you want your money back?'

Well, obviously I really wanted my money back, but by this time I harboured so much resentment for him because it was a particularly difficult time for business. I said: 'Well, I want him in jail,' and they said if the court knew he was going to pay me back, he could escape prison. He had offered to remortgage his house. It was something like £100,000, so I got my money back and kept the £20,000, but the time and energy it took to focus on something like that was enormous.

Clubs can be a constant source of entertainment for all sorts of reasons. Five years ago, we had an amazing incident at Space. We were advertising for staff and a young lad was being interviewed. It was early in the morning and suddenly three or four guys with hoods over their heads burst in, bundled him into the office and ordered Michael the manager to open the safe. The outcome was that both Michael and the young lad were tied to a chair. The villains pinched the money and then scarpered. Eventually, someone found the two victims and they were untied. The manager said to this young lad: 'I don't suppose you still want a job here after all that then, do you?' He said: 'Yes, I do. It's exciting!'

* * * * *

Louise does the accounts at the remaining two nightclubs, the Birdcage in Manchester and Space in Leeds. I deal with the advertising, while she handles the drag queens. We make a good team, but clubs have become a much smaller part of my life in recent years, as you might imagine.

CHAPTER NINE

EVERYTHING'S £1

My Las Vegas experience projected me into the heady world of running nightclubs with such force and enthusiasm that naturally the shops took a bit of a backseat for a while. I still loved the retail world just as passionately, but once we got to three shops we hit a bit of a roadblock.

With hindsight, we were fortunate to establish those first three shops. The chance to establish our original Wakefield store came from a rare decision by a local authority to offer a retail opportunity. I just happened to be in the right place at the right time to take advantage and I was lucky. When the local NatWest bank manager Mr Shackleton agreed to lend me the cash I needed to get the shop off the ground, I was equally fortunate.

The Bradford breakthrough came about because the city was slightly in disarray, thanks to the massive redevelopment that was just starting at the time. If my brother hadn't been making a rare trip to the city when he spotted the potential of a large empty shop there, then I'm sure someone else would have moved in. Once again, I was lucky.

Our third shop in Barnsley was previously owned by one of my wholesalers. After discovering it was going to be available, I was able to make a direct contact and quickly do a deal. In those days getting a shop was not nearly so easy as today and running nightclubs slowed me down as a person and changed my focus for quite a while. I was constantly looking for new shops to grow the retail business, but it really was difficult: you had to have what they called a 'good covenant'. It wasn't a case of simply wanting the premises and being prepared to pay the rent. The agents representing the landlords would ask: 'Who are you?' and 'What's your background?' They would ask questions like: 'What kind of funding have you got?' and 'What sort of bank account do you have?'

In those days, before all the retail parks cropped up, space on the high street was at a premium. It was a very different scene from today. Once we got to three shops, we were trying to find a fourth but it proved impossible; we kept coming up against those covenant problems. If someone with an established name and reputation like Next or Argos wanted to open a new branch and we wanted to take over the same premises, we were never going to get it. It was very frustrating, but that was the way it was.

I'm a market man, really, and that's the way I was seen. The company we had was regarded as so small that at the time I didn't carry any weight in the boardrooms of those who ran the property companies. The long, losing battle to find that fourth shop was certainly part of the reason behind my involvement with the clubs; it wasn't just having my head turned by the glitz and glamour of Las Vegas. So for quite a few years we had three shops and two nightclubs – I think we ran like that for five years at least.

There was no grand business plan; I just ran the two separate businesses at the same time and it seemed to work. One year, the shops would be showing prominence and making money and the clubs would be struggling; the next year it would frequently be the other way round. The two enterprises helped support each other, I found. I was a lot younger then and I think I thrived on the constant switching of concentration. Some years they would both do well and I would get both businesses making good money. That was like utopia, but somehow it never lasted. I would think, 'This is fantastic!' then all of a sudden a club would drop off and I would have to find the funds to refurbish it and be forced into borrowing a bit of money from here and there. For quite a few years business was nothing like it is now. My brother Laurie was quite prominent in running those three stores with me but it always seemed to me that I had a 'second job' running two nightclubs.

I was always on the lookout for new shops and after a while I managed to get three more at once from the liquidation of Wentworth Mills. Yorkshire-based, they had a shop in Sheffield, one in Ilkeston and another in Salford. It was not easy but somehow we managed to buy them from the receiver. That doubled our size at a stroke from three to six shops; it was a big change. I took over the leasehold and it really helped us to increase the all-important cash flow.

Later, we took over a couple of shops in Preston because thanks to this expansion, our covenant was seen to be getting better. If you go to a landlord and say you have six shops and you've been in business for ten years, it sounds as if you are a serious operator. Landlords can look at your accounts for the previous three years and see for themselves that your financial strength is building and you're not just some flash fly-by-night.

We were still trading as Bargain Centre. Then there was a widespread move to ease a little upmarket. People seemed to be starting to trade up, at least that was the clear impression we had. There was more money about so we tried to trade up and we changed some of the shops to a very upmarket look, with timber fronts and neon signs saying 'Everyday Things'. But it didn't work to any great extent; we never really got any more successful than where we were with the Bargain Centre. It was the most successful brand we had until we started with a single price. That was in 1995 when we opened our first single-price format store under the brand name of 'Everything's £1'.

I've never pretended it was the most original idea in the world but I had seen the early days of Poundland and they certainly gave me food for thought. Years before, people on the market had done similar things, selling everything for a pound, but no one had ever taken it into a heavy commercial enterprise. In many ways, Steve Smith, who ran Poundland, was a trailblazer. I looked at the single price and I thought, 'I think I'll have a go at this.' So we transferred some of our shops over, though we were still only buying from wholesalers. We changed three of our Bargain Centre shops to single price, naming them 'Everything's £1'. I had big yellow signs made to try and hammer home the single-price message and in those days it seemed to work so we changed over another three shops. The takings were higher, the margins were tighter, and it seemed to give us a better cash flow. But that was before we got into imports so the margin was still very, very tight because we were buying all the pound stuff from wholesalers who had imported it from overseas. I know now that to make the pound game really work, you have got to be importing goods yourself. We never ever thought we would get to that level when I changed over the shops, though.

My son Christopher has always been very interested in retailing in general and our business in particular. Even when he was at school, he showed that he had inherited the ability to buy and sell and make a profit. When he was as young as ten or eleven, he would enthusiastically go to car boot sales with my mother, but I'll let him tell his own story a little later. It was in 1997 when Christopher was just fifteen that I took the first step on a journey to China that was to galvanise my whole business. I think it was just a hunch at the time but as I prepared to make this first exploratory journey, I decided I wanted to take my son with me.

Poundland had grown to around forty or fifty shops by this time and seemed to have found a winning formula. I knew much of their stock was coming from China and then I received an interesting approach from an old friend of mine called Simon Heginbotham, who had been doing some business on the import side with Poundland. 'Have you ever thought about importing?' he asked. Intrigued, I said: 'I don't think we're equipped.' 'Come to China and see. I'll show you,' he suggested.

Simon, whose father Stafford Heginbotham was once chairman of Bradford City, was very experienced in sourcing goods in volume from China. I knew that much of Poundland's success was a consequence of importing in volume from China and the Far East, helped by Simon. Although Christopher was young, I was well aware that he had wanted to be in the shops from the age of seven. He had always wanted to sell. I was convinced my son would benefit from the experience and even then, I valued his potential input, so I decided to accept Simon's invitation and to take him with me. He might have seemed too youthful to involve but I remembered my own early market experiences, which had always stood me in good stead.

Christopher was keen to come with Simon and me to Hong Kong and China so we went to the high school and I asked permission for him to have time off school for the trip. But they were not at all keen on the idea and they were none too helpful. This was long before the days when parents found themselves fined for taking their children on holiday in term time and it was by no means a holiday. I said: 'Look, with respect, he's fifteen years old and he has already told me very clearly that he does not want to stay on at school after he reaches sixteen. He wants to come into the family business so this seems an ideal opportunity for him to find out more about his future.' The school was still not happy, but he came on the trip.

So we went there and had a look and even at fifteen, Christopher had a hell of a lot to contribute because he had been in and out of our shops since he was born. He was interested in new products and prices and the whole future of the retail world. For me, he was a big bonus: even at a young age he often gave me wise advice, which can be extremely helpful when you are a bit unsure. When you are controlling very tight purse strings you have to be careful what you are doing, and he had an excellent attitude to it right from the early days.

The trip went very well indeed. Even though we were going to the Far East for the first time, we didn't have time to see any of the tourist sites; we were just too busy. My son and I learned a lot and he made a great contribution. In fact, soon afterwards Simon suggested we visit a clearance show in New York to buy stock. This was while we were changing over the shops to single price. Again, I decided to take Christopher with me. I've always kept him involved from a young age in the same way my own dad kept me involved in the business when I was a young boy – I suppose I tried to replicate my own upbringing in a different kind of way. Christopher came with me to New York and Simon brought along with him a very bright young man in his early thirties called Mark Ward, who worked for him in the discount business as an importer.

Christopher was fifteen by the time the four of us made the trip to New York. Again, I will let him describe it for himself later, but my memory is that we learned a great deal despite struggling to disguise my son's youth! He wasn't very tall and in America, the age limits were stricter for everything: you had to be twenty-one to drink in a bar. To attend the trade shows you had to be over eighteen, I think, so he still didn't quite qualify. We had to tell him to get on his tiptoes to go through! Sandwiched between us, we got him in to see the show and it was well worth the effort. Christopher was very, very hungry, even at a young age, and made some valuable contributions, as did Mark Ward. Their two ambitious younger minds seemed full of ideas and in turn their enthusiasm gave me a lift.

Simon confided in me that while Mark had been with him for several years, his business was not doing as well as in previous years and times were hard. He told me: 'Mark is probably ready to have a change from me because I can't really afford to fund his wages anymore.' So I had a talk with Mark and explained we had plans to expand and how we were in the middle of changing our outlets over to single-price shops. He seemed a bright young man and so I invited him to join us for a three-month trial. It turned out well and he's still with us all these years later, only now he's on the board. He was really more of a salesman than an importer; in those days, Simon was the importer.

Previously, Mark used to work with a guy called Phil Butterworth, who would buy stock for the little cranes that people put money in to try and grab a key ring or whatever in amusement halls around the seaside towns. Customers usually fail to grab a prize, but Phil grabbed plenty of money supplying the attractive little goodies inside. Through nights out with Simon in Hong Kong and China, he became a friend of mine and eventually got involved with the popular kids' TV character Bob the Builder.

It was all licensed stuff but Phil thought, 'Why should I bother with a licence? It's all available in China. They'll make it for me and I'll ship it in direct.' He was short of space to store some of his stock and so I put him in touch with a good friend of mine, Terry Padgett, who is a toy importer. Terry always had surplus space in his warehouse and over the years we've rented some of it ourselves from time to time. We had stopped using it because by then we had our own established warehouse. Terry rang me one day and said if I ever knew of anyone who wanted space he would be pleased for me to put them in touch. Phil Butterworth just happened to say to me in passing: 'I need some warehouse space.' Naturally, I put him in touch with Terry and thought no more of it.

Phil didn't tell me what he wanted to put in it, but I later learned it was Bob the Builder stuff. He rented the space in Terry's warehouse in Barnsley. As I've said, I introduced them but then forgot all about it. Phil did the deal with Terry and then, about six weeks later, Terry rang me, quite irate, and said: 'What the hell have you done to me?' I couldn't understand what he was on about. 'I've got Customs and Excise swarming all over my building!' he said. It turned out that Phil was in serious trouble with the authorities and ended up doing time for that import. While waiting to go for trial, he made a visit to the Birdcage in Leeds to see me. I had told the drag queen DJ there about Phil's trouble over Bob the Builder. Of course when he walked in, the DJ started playing the famous song, which was a bit of a sore point! Phil was confident he was not going to go inside so we all had a big laugh. Unfortunately for him, he was wrong about the verdict.

Not long later, when he was sixteen, my son Christopher left school and came straight into the family business. From day one he has been absolutely brilliant! Mark and Chris – the two young people on that trip to New York – along with my brother Laurie, would become my key pillars of support in running Poundworld.

CHAPTER TEN

CHINA AND THE FAR EAST

Importing stock from China has helped to transform our business, yet my first impression of the country hardly encouraged me to think it would alter our future so comprehensively. The China I first visited in 1997 was quite different to today. In those earlier days there were far more bikes than cars on the roads. I was amazed that one guy could get his whole family, a fridge and a freezer on a single bike – it was unbelievable! In just about every way, they seemed to be years, decades even, behind us. The hotels were primitive and distinctly unwelcoming. It wasn't all mud huts but in my early visits, I would see a high-rise building and normally, it would be surrounded by much older, often colonial-style buildings, even some shacks. Now it's completely different: all the shacks have gone and the cities are the most modern and cosmopolitan you could ever imagine. My later visits have been to Shanghai, where there was always a strong British presence, and the influence is still there in some of the buildings. A brilliantly vibrant place to do business and full of contrasts, it's a wonderful city.

My friend Simon Heginbotham was very helpful in introducing me to China and the Far East. He had a partner called Carloo and together they had a company called Simcar. When we went over to Hong Kong they were an agency and so we signed up with them: they bought the goods for us and put a percentage on it. We agreed, but the trick to making a success of importing from China, or anywhere else come to that, is to make sure you get the figures right, although it's hard to estimate values and profit margins beforehand.

This was when I received one of many business lessons from my precocious young son. There were two ways of paying for the goods we bought, either at the exchange rate on the day they were shipped or at a predicted future rate agreed on the day of the deal. 'Safety first, let's go for the predicted rate. Then at least we know where we are,' I thought.

In those days our business wasn't a big corporate monster, I was just making sure I was getting my wages. By then it was ingrained in me that your living always has to stay intact. In fact, I later realised that I showed Christopher my cautious side, just as my own dad had always shown me his cautious side when I was pushing him. When you're completely responsible for paying the mortgage, you have to be very careful with your money, though. So I was always looking for the less risky option while my son was probably looking at it more rationally, even though he was only around fifteen years old at the time. I said I thought we would take their predicted exchange rate and he told me: 'You're a fool.' His argument was that if they had to predict the exchange rate, they would have to put a lot on to be sure of making a good profit. 'They are not going to run it too close, they are going to put money on it,' he argued. 'You're right, but don't you think we should know exactly what we're paying?' I said. 'No, we should risk it. They're going to price up to cover themselves so we'll be paying a higher price,' he told me. He convinced me to be bolder and all the way through, we took the risk on the exchange rate and over the years it paid off. Sometimes you have to allow yourself to be overruled, even if you are the boss. That wasn't our first disagreement, and it certainly won't be the last, but it was one of the most memorable.

The early visits to the Far East were a great learning process. When we first went there, we went to Simcar's office in Hong Kong. There were a lot of factories everywhere and we visited one or two of them. We were not quite so confident or driven then and so we allowed ourselves to be led by Simon and Carloo. It worked out well enough for the first two or three years. I could see the potential for our business because buying stuff there increased the margins quite considerably.

Representatives from many of the factories used to visit Simcar's office. They would come with examples of their wares, we would sit round the table and they would say: 'We've got this.' One of my most frequent comments was that it was like seeing a lot of old friends. I would see stuff I had bought from wholesalers in Britain for 55 pence and it would be for sale here to us for 25 pence. It was exciting! Immediately, I could see the potential for significant profit increases. After shipping, that item probably landed in the UK at 35 to 40 pence to us, which was still a substantial saving. All the bells started ringing. I was half aware this was what would happen. I'd been in the business a long time and I was expecting to see some reductions, but I still got quite a surprise. I realised the potential increase in profits with some enthusiasm. And if you bought large quantities, the price per item went down considerably. With extra volume, it was remarkable how cheaply you could get things. We did see right away that there was great potential if we worked with Simcar.

My association with Simon Heginbotham came about largely because his relationship with Poundland had seriously deteriorated. It seems that Simon, who had more or less introduced Poundland to the Far East, found he was no longer wanted. Eventually, Poundland dispensed with his services, which is why he came to us. He told me himself the reason they let him go was that he had become rather too fond of the entertaining side of his work in Hong Kong and China. What happened with them, and sadly, what later happened with us, was they tired of his easy-going attitude and lack of discipline. Although very knowledgeable in the import business and in many ways ahead of his time, he was unfortunately his own worst enemy. I'm still in contact with him and quite recently, enjoyed a night out with him. As a friend he's good company, but he can be difficult to work with.

Anyway, Poundland had three or four years of importing so they knew they could find their way round and they got involved with another company called PMS, a large wholesaler and importer in England with a big office in Hong Kong. Retailers like me can go into the PMS showroom, buy from them and then import the goods to Britain but we would still be paying a middleman, and key to the success of what we do is that to make the maximum profit, sooner or later you've got to get rid of the middleman.

Simon came to us and after three years, even Carloo, who was his partner, was fed up with him. Carloo was a huge man, the biggest Chinaman you've ever seen, but he was a soft kind of guy and a proper gentleman. One day he came to me and said in his broken English: 'I'm sick of Simon. If me and Simon go our separate ways, will you still do business with me?'

And I agreed. It was not a difficult decision because he was the key man who did all the work. So we ended our relationship with Simon and took on Carloo. To begin with, we agreed on a deal with a tighter commission and that went on for another two or three years. By then Poundworld was running harder and faster and so we told Carloo that we could not afford to pay the commission any longer and we would have to take over the business, pay his office rent and his staff salaries. We offered to pay his wages and again a smaller commission. That worked for a while, then more efficiency measures had to be put in place. What happened really was that we outgrew Carloo's set-up. We needed more sophistication with our software that Carloo could not provide.

At the same time we took on someone else, Billy Singh, who is based in Shanghai. He's a great guy and an unusual character to say the least. Early on, Billy identified that a lot of the factories were moving from Hong Kong to China and of course as we have since seen, China was becoming very strong economically. When I came back from one of the first trips, someone asked me what China was like as a country. 'Eventually they're going to take over the world,' I predicted.

Today, that's proving to be true and I said that more than fifteen years ago. Now the Chinese are pulling the strings and seem to be manipulating everything.

Anyway, Billy used to work for PMS, the large importing company. He had no retail experience, but he knew stock because he used to buy it. It was a good basis for us to start. Instead of having to go and visit factories and do lots of investigative work, he knew all the factories and could visit and negotiate prices for a lot of similar items, as he had been doing so for his previous employer. Billy started working from home and going round all of the factories, doing the sourcing and everything necessary. Eventually we opened a small office just on the outskirts of Shanghai and only six months ago we moved to a big office and showroom in the centre of the city. I've been there twice in the time we've had it and it gives us a substantial presence.

We were very impressed when we first used to visit the big factories in China, with their smart showrooms and offices. Well, now we've got exactly the same! The reason we had to move from the small office we had was that Billy initially used to work from home and then from a small office about an hour's drive out of Shanghai, not far from where he lived. He urged us to recruit more staff because the Poundworld momentum was growing. By this time we'd gone from 50 to 100 shops.

Christopher and I made several trips to China – he even went with his grandmother once! I think he must have been about twenty when he started going on his own. What sparked this was that on one particular trip my son and I had seats booked and at the last minute I couldn't go. I was given a message that

I had to be in court in person, where there was a big issue on licensing over the Birdcage in Leeds. The solicitor advised me that if I didn't want to lose my licence then I should appear to give evidence in person. That meant Christopher would have to go to China on his own. I didn't feel comfortable with this, but of course we had my ticket. We used to travel on Upper Class with Virgin. Christopher was happy to go on his own, but I rang my mother and of course she said instantly that she would go in my place. Christopher had said OK, so I rang Mum and told her it would be a bit of a rush. Typically, she just said: 'I'll be ready.'

The great thing was that the Chinese are very respectful of older people so my mother was treated wonderfully. She and my son visited two or three factories a day and they showed Mum enormous respect. Whichever city or province they visited she was wined and dined regally. She was well into her late seventies when she went and the trip was a great success. My mum loved it.

* * * * *

For me it was very difficult to bring an end to our relationship with Carloo. He is a good man and we had become friends, but sometimes in business you have to set friendship to one side and do what's best for the bottom line. To come up to date with our operation in China, we closed the Hong Kong office two years ago. It became quite obvious something was wrong. As Billy Singh put it: 'Carloo can't keep pace with me, he can't give me the answers.'

By this time Billy was doing the sourcing and the Hong Kong office was looking after the shipping and tracking of the stock with factories. The difference was that Billy is an automated person with up-to-date computer systems and Carloo was very old-fashioned. When you went into Carloo's office, he'd have eight people and every desk would have a huge pile of papers on it, but when you saw Billy, it was all happening on a computer. Typically, my son Christopher swiftly identified the problem and told me flatly: 'Dad, we can't carry on with Carloo.'

By this time Carloo and me had become very good friends, though perhaps only on a business level. Christopher had also become close to him. As a twenty-year-old, he used to travel to China on his own and Carloo would meet him at the airport. He would take him round the shows and then put him back on the plane home. I always knew my son was in safe hands because Carloo was a very responsible person, a first-class gentleman. Everything you would want in a friend, he was someone you could rely on. That's why it was very difficult for me to break our relationship off after at least fifteen years. Christopher grew up in the business and very quickly got a handle on the importing side. This led to the situation about two years ago.

Anyway, Billy was putting systems in and Carloo couldn't keep pace. I had to go over and talk to him about closing the office. After such a long time that was very hard. I trusted Carloo 100 per cent, but he had one, or possibly two, understudies that I never had quite the same kind of relationship with. Crucially, they shared all the knowledge we had built up, so I had to be sure that knowledge wasn't going to go to our rivals. One of them was a nice lad, but he had a wife and family to look after, so he could have gone into survival mode and taken some of our commercial secrets straight to the opposition. He would not have done so maliciously, I'm sure, but he might have been desperate to help himself so I had to be very careful and discreet while closing Carloo's office down.

Carloo was OK, but it was brutal and unpleasant. I had to walk in and say: 'Stop what you're doing now.' We owed him twelve months commission so I said: 'I'll pay you every penny I owe you and I'll pay you over the next twelve months.' I felt very guilty and then I backed down a little. I went in, intending to commandeer the office, but Carloo was looking at me and saying: 'What is going on?' Very quickly, I got a guilty conscience and I said: 'Stop, we're not doing it like this, this is not what's happening!' I asked Carloo if I could talk to him in private so we went into his office and I explained that I was going to pay him what I owed him but that our business relationship was over.

He was a little upset but we talked about it and we got over it. It was quite an emotional thing, to be honest. To cut a long story short, we shook hands after we had been there for three days and had made sure that the understudies could not do us any harm and nothing could be leaked because now Poundland and 99p Store are out there in China. Our competitors are there and the employees could have been very useful for them, just to guide them where we'd been going. Whether or not they would have been interested, I don't know, but we couldn't take the risk.

In fact, Carloo took the news well. 'Me and you will always be brothers,' he told me. From a big Chinaman, this was quite touching and very emotional too. I said: 'In twelve months, Carloo, I don't know where our business is going, but I might come back to you because I have some other ideas. You're going to get your commission for twelve months, whether you come into work or not. That's up to you. I just want to make sure you get where you want to be.'

About eight months later I rang Carloo and said I was coming to one of the extra shows to have a look round by myself. I offered to pay him extra if he would walk round with me, with a view to trying to crank up some kind of business with him because he still had the operation and I knew how hard it was. We could have utilised that operation in some other way, but unfortunately it didn't really work out so our relationship petered out about eighteen months ago when he was finally paid up. But I did see him again and we had three or four days together round a show in China and got on great so we finished the deal honourably.

As soon as I visited the China and the Far East, I knew this would radically alter my business. When you see the prices, the potential is obvious; it was just moulding those prices into an opportunity. And obviously, the opportunity we had was a single-price range of products, with everything high quality, but bought very, very cheaply.

You can't sell inferior products because if you do, you don't have a business.

CHAPTER ELEVEN

FAMILY MATTERS

My brother Laurie has decided to retire, now that the sale of the company has gone through. I'm really going to miss him because we've been working together since we were young kids. Just because I feel differently and intend to carry on working doesn't mean I don't understand how my brother feels. Besides, he's worked very hard and he certainly deserves his retirement. I think he will enjoy it; already in his first three months, he's had three holidays! It'll just be very strange not seeing him every day after all the years together and I'm sorry he's leaving. Laurie shares some of his feelings here.

Laurie Edwards says: 'It's always been great to have a big brother, especially one like Chris. We were very close, growing up, and we still are. It's been great working with him and I'm still amazed by his drive and energy. We're not the same in that department – I don't mind hard work, but I like eight or preferably ten hours' sleep a night, while Chris hardly seems to need any!

'As kids, I always thought it was exciting to live in a wagon and keep moving around. It was like one great big family, where everyone pitched in and got on. I think we did little jobs right from the time we could walk and talk. I've always liked dealing with the public and whether it's fairgrounds or markets or shops, you've got to get on well with people if you want to do well. Our dad taught us very early on in life that when it comes to handling customers, a smile goes a long way.

'Dad was a huge influence on Chris and me. He was very strict with us and always kept us under control. A tremendously hard worker, he showed us by example how we should behave. He never hit us, but we daren't do anything wrong. His standards were high and he expected us to live up to them. I try to bring my own kids up the way he brought us up. I've always tried to copy the way he lived his life: he liked a drink with good friends, but he was first and foremost a family man.

'We all did all we could for the family business. Among my earliest memories is rushing home from junior school, the old cathedral school in Wakefield, to help my mum and dad pack up the stall. I would much rather have been out playing football, but we

knew where our loyalties were, even when we were very young.

'Chris was a great big brother, especially in those years when the age difference was so much more important. We were always close. I remember when I was fourteen being taken to the Fiesta Club at Stockton to see Morecambe & Wise. I could only go because I was with Chris and Billy Crow and some other friends. Billy's uncle was always in the clubs and we used to go and say: 'Uncle Stanley sent us,' and they would put us in the front seats because Uncle Stanley used to go in, spending a lot of money. He was a bit of a character. Dad wouldn't have let me go on my own. Chris would have been seventeen then, so it was OK. He took me on quite a few things. Chris always protected me when I was younger; he was always there for me. We've had our differences over the years and many a set-to, right up to the present day. What our dad always said is: "If you've got your brother with you, you can have your fights and arguments, but you're always going to be brothers."

'I think most lads we knew in Wakefield thought we were well off, but we never seemed too affluent to me! It was a normal, happy childhood. As I grew up, the business graduated from fairgrounds to markets. Dad realised fairgrounds were fading out and it became more difficult to do both. As the markets got busier, you had to be there to keep your stall and he realised it was only the big, main fairs

where you could do well. In many ways markets are very similar to fairs. They are certainly operated by similar people so I don't think it was much of a culture change moving between the two worlds. They are mainly all good, hard-working people. In many ways, it was all an excellent preparation for Poundworld! Chris and I both handled money from the age of five and knew all about meeting and dealing with all sorts of different people from a young age. They are the key skills and it was a great start in life to learn them early.

'Dad passed all his buying skills down to Chris and me as soon as we were old enough to understand. Knowing the value of something is the hardest thing to learn. It was never an easy life, but I never minded that. I think the markets could be the toughest. When you woke up on a Saturday morning, with the rain hitting the bedroom windows, you certainly knew you were in for a tough day – the shop was much drier! I liked it from that point of view. Chris was always very ambitious to move on; he was always looking for the next thing. I suppose it was originally Dad's idea to keep everything in the family but that has become the Dad philosophy of all of us: we all know it's better to be in it together. It's been great to be in business with my brother.

'Finding new shops was much more difficult when we were starting. You need a little bit of luck and I think we were fortunate when I went to Bradford to get a suit to get married in and spotted

this shop that looked full of potential for us. Chris always said: "If you see any good shops on the high street, let me know!" It was just near the bus station and the new Arndale Centre that was being built then and a McDonald's was opening three shops away. I told Chris and he started negotiations. We managed to get it and it was a huge step forward. The Bradford shop was much bigger than our first shop in Wakefield so we could let some space off, and my mum even had a café!

'Then we got a third shop in Barnsley and ran like that for quite a while. Chris started to buy nightclubs then, but I never wanted to get involved in that business. I did go and help a little sometimes and if my dad was away on holiday, I would go and do the door, taking the money. Chris had some good clubs, but I never wanted to be a part of them. I definitely realised I didn't have his energy then – I don't really understand how he's always so full of energy on so little sleep.

'Eventually we started to get more shops. We opened in Salford, Worksop and Ilkeston, though we came out of Ilkeston after there was some trouble with the landlord. We bought quite a few shops from the receivers and built up to a chain of about ten shops. It was a good business and we had a warehouse at Ouzlewell Green. At the time it seemed really big and it was quite an important step forward. In the early days I used to do a lot of the deliveries myself, but we set on a growing number of drivers. In the early

days, of course, Chris and I did just about everything ourselves; I have fond memories of the days when I'd just put stuff in the van and head out on the road. There were a few iffy moments along the way but we always made it. Now we've got eighty-five drivers on our books! It's amazing; I can remember when two were a nightmare! And ten years ago, we had three people in the offices. Now it's like the Eighth Army out there!

'As well as working together all our lives, Chris and I also spent a lot of time playing football together. For years, we played for the Showmen's Guild teams. We played for Yorkshire and for the England Guild; we played the Scotland Guild at Meadowbank stadium and we used to play at Elland Road as well. Football was something we both enjoyed very much, but it wasn't always easy to combine it with work. I used to get up very early on Sunday mornings in the old days and get into our little van and go to Bradford, picking up a couple of lads on the way. We would fill the van up, go back to Barnsley and unload it in the shop, ready for the girls to come in on Monday morning. Then I went to Leeds to play football at half past ten. After one match I remember the manager saying: "You weren't your normal self this morning." "No," I said. "I've been up since one o'clock in the morning."

'Chris was a good player, but his timekeeping wasn't always too great. We were once going to play for the Yorkshire Showmen's Guild against the North

Above and centre: Grandma on the original stall which was on Wakefield Market.

Below: Saltburn-by-the-Sea, the seaside town where I was born.

Left: My mother's hot dog and hamburger stall at the market. It was a successful little business.

Right: Fairground stalls – a rifle range with *(from left to right)* me, Mum, Dad and Laurie.

Chris Johnson and Son's Noah's Ark at Harrogate.

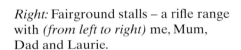

Below: One of the valuable fairground rides that my family lost when all of our wealth was left to one person who then left the business.

Left and below: My son, Christopher, alongside my mother, working hard on their car boot business.

Below: Steam engine Betty who tragically claimed a young life.

Above: Sonya and Nicola – no prizes for coming second. They won all the cups at their junior school sports and I won a pen for the Father's Race!

Below: This was my great-great-grandad who was a once a daring trapeze artist, though it looks like his days on the high wire are over here.

Left: Me and Miss Orry!

Right: Alongside three drag queens.

Left: A troupe of glamorous dancers at the Birdcage.

Above: Dollars, the giant nightclub I risked so much to buy.

Below: The EastEnder Anita Dobson leaves Albert Square to visit Dollars.

Above: A visit to China with my son Christopher, Simon Heginbotham, who introduced us to the Far East, and Carloo, who was such a big help in our early days of importing.

Below: Mum and Dad. Happy times at a wedding in February 1987.

Above: A lorry and wagon going through Stokesley town centre – our family home!

Below: An aerial shot of a house I'm buying – it's a long way from living in a wagon!

of England. I think all the other players went on a coach, but Chris and I were driving. It was three hours before the kick-off and he rings me from Manchester: "I'm leaving here in a minute and I'll pick you up and we'll go up to Durham." Before all the road improvements this was a long and difficult journey. We shot off to the ground at Durham University and just got there about five minutes before kick-off. All the others were waiting and the coach gave us both a real earful. Chris has always been like that with his time, trying to fit more into the day than there are hours. He's in such a hurry that very often he doesn't leave himself enough time.

'The recent success takes your breath away. We couldn't have stopped at three or even ten shops because we needed more buying power. We have been opening forty or fifty shops a year for the last four or five years. The old days seem like another world. I think it was the recession that catapulted us forward. Before the tough times, the powers that be didn't want pound shops in town centres – I think they thought we lowered the tone! Now they see how sharp and popular our shops can be, they've changed their minds. People gradually realised we were a credit to any shopping centre. Now I think we've earned our success and people go to the pound shops first and then go to the supermarket.

'There are downsides to every business, of course, and one of the persistent problems that upsets me is dishonesty. Shoplifting by customers and stealing

by employees is a constant problem. With the employment laws as they are today, you can't say anything to anybody. When we started, you could sack somebody on the spot for dishonesty or for not doing their job but you can't do that today. You can catch them pinching out of your till but you still can't chuck them straight out of the door.

'The police don't look on shoplifting as a crime any more; sometimes they won't even attend. Chris has complained to the police over the years, but there is always only so much we can do. I get upset with some of the modern attitudes to hard work. Most of our employees are great, but you're bound to get the odd shirker. The excuses they use to explain not turning up make my blood boil. Many of them have had several grandparents die in a very short time and the other day one young lad said he wasn't coming in to work because he had "been up all night with my upset girlfriend". Our book of excuses would be a bestseller!

'The shifting fashions of what sells in our shops is fascinating. When yo-yos briefly returned to popularity, we simply couldn't get enough of them, particularly in our little shop in Huddersfield. We had a very good girl in charge there called Keira, who kept pleading with me to deliver more. I went over specially on a Saturday morning with 870 yo-yos and I'd only just got back to the warehouse when Keira was on the phone to say she'd sold them all! This year it's loom bands, but unfortunately these trends are not so easy to spot in advance.

'The Frozen *merchandise certainly leapt off the shelves. Customers were buying as much as they could and then selling it on eBay! A security guard even had to separate two women fighting over the stuff. A lot of our goods are such great value people can go into our shops and buy stuff and sell it on again. Some of our hardware products are even better than the branded makes according to some of our happy customers. We sell thousands of screwdrivers and people buy our paintbrushes because they can afford to throw them away instead of cleaning them.*

'*I think I have more sympathy with the people running our shops than Chris. He gets very upset when everything doesn't look just right, but I realise our employees are busy and can't always find time to fill up. Working in the family business all my life has been great; I wouldn't change anything for the world. Chris has always been a brilliant big brother. His energy is amazing. I keep telling him to remember how old he is, but I don't think he listens!*

'*Tragically, my dad died from a heart attack before this recent major push of expansions. It was a shock that took the whole family by surprise, and one I don't think I've ever quite recovered from. He was on holiday in Florida when it happened, which somehow made it feel worse. I'll let my mum relate the sad details.*'

Alice Edwards says: '*My husband Chris was only sixty-nine years old when he died and he left a huge hole in all our lives. It was horribly sudden. We were spending a few days in Orlando with some friends when he said he didn't feel too good. First, he asked for indigestion tablets and then he had a bath, but he still wasn't right. We went to Universal Studios and it was very hot. I was blaming the sun for making him ill and tried to get him to buy a hat. He refused, saying: "If you think I'm paying that much for a silly Donald Duck hat, you've got another thing coming!" But then he said: "Come on, let's get out of here. I don't feel so good."*

'They were the last words he spoke; he just collapsed. We got an ambulance and they rushed him to the hospital. I just remember sitting in this room waiting and a doctor coming up and saying: "We are doing everything we can." It took me a long time to recover, but you never really get over it. Hardly a day goes by without my husband being mentioned. He is still sorely missed both by family and friends. It was very sad and such a shock to lose him. No one in the showmen's fraternity could believe it.'

It was a terrible time for the whole family and I felt it very deeply, but for me there was to be a lesson in my dad's death. Naturally, I talked a lot to my mum about what had happened and I came to know the build-up to Dad's fatal heart attack in detail. Before then we didn't have the education to know that he was building up to having major heart problems. About seven years ago that knowledge of what had happened to my dad was so important.

It was an ordinary day and Laurie and I were in our warehouse at Birstall in Leicestershire, which is now our overspill warehouse. As a consequence of playing countless games of football and having a bad hip, my brother always walks a little strangely, but he looked worse than normal. I asked if he was all right and his reply really shocked me. He said: 'My chest hurts a bit.'

Instantly, I recalled how my mother had described what had happened to our dad. I offered him a cup of tea, but he preferred water. He had a glass of water and I made him talk me through how he was feeling but he was anxious to play it down: he had a bit of indigestion, he thought. It all sounded frighteningly like what had happened to Dad, so I said: 'Come on, let's get you to hospital.' I told him to get in the car and I'd take him to Pinderfields Hospital in Wakefield. But Laurie was not very keen on the idea. 'What if it's nothing?' he said. 'Only me and you know about it,' I told him. 'We're not going to tell anyone if it is nothing to worry about.' He said: 'I don't want anyone thinking I'm soft.' I quickly persuaded him to do as I said and got him in the car. So I drove to the hospital, dropped him off at A&E and went to park. When I came back, he'd gone: he was already in a bed in the casualty area, but he was still talking. I was relieved, but then the medics told me they were transferring him to Leeds because they thought he was having a heart attack.

Laurie said: 'You'd better tell Margaret.' So I rang his wife to explain. I warned her not to panic and told her what had happened. He was being transferred to Leeds General Infirmary because they could deal with him there. The outcome was that he had a stent put in and they corrected his problem. He was having a heart attack when I first noticed he wasn't walking properly. If I hadn't known of my father's experience I'd have probably said: 'Pull yourself together, you nutcase! Get on with it!' It was just that the feelings that Laurie described sounded so familiar after listening to my mum talking about my dad's death.

I've since learned that often people suffering heart problems go into denial when they experience the initial symptoms and that is what Laurie did. I can only advise anyone who goes through anything remotely similar to seek help straight away; I know I will.

I've talked a lot about my son Christopher because he's so involved in the business but my two daughters, Nicola and Sonya, are just as close to my heart. They are both busy mothers now, but when they were younger Nicola passed a lot of exams and did well at school, while Sonya, my younger daughter, who people often say is very much like me, wasn't at all academic. She couldn't wait to get out of school, but she has done very well in business. After leaving school at sixteen, she decided she didn't want a job with me: she wanted to be a beauty therapist.

Nicola stayed on until she was eighteen so they left school at around the same time. They started college together, training to be beauty therapists. After gaining work experience independently, they opened their own salon. They ran that business very successfully for ten or twelve years. Their mother was the receptionist so it was another family affair. I was impressed by how well they did. In the first place they came to me with all their projections. Although I'd said I would finance them initially, I was thinking they were going to get a little shop somewhere with two cubicles. Then they came with this info on an old mill in a beauty spot near Wakefield. It had been a pub/restaurant that had gone bankrupt and closed down and they said: 'This will make an ideal place.' It was a long way from being a little shop! So I negotiated with the receiver and I managed to buy the place for £205,000. I expected to spend about fifteen grand for that to be kitted out with all the gym stuff and other equipment.

It was an investment I've never regretted and it was one of the best moves I've ever made because it took them from being teenagers to grown successful women. Twelve years later and one grandchild had arrived and everyone shared looking after the baby while the salon was going. It opened in 1995 and closed in 2007. They actually sold up, made a massive profit and paid me back my investment. It was a very good move.

Now they just spend most of their time looking after their families, although Sonya is back at work again: she has three children now, and she is selling on the Internet. She has got the genes. Academically, Nicola is probably most clever of the two, but Sonya is showing all the traits of being like me. Nicola is bright, too and sometimes Sonya uses her sister as a sounding board, and they are working together again on this internet selling.

They don't want to come into Poundworld. At times they have both worked for me when they were younger, but now they want to be independent. They are great kids. I tried to model their upbringing and Chris's on the upbringing I myself had. There was no pocket money handed out without jobs being completed to earn it. From a young age, even when they were still at school, on a Saturday they had to go to work in one of our shops to get their pocket money. They might have got a bit more pocket money than the average kid, but they still had to work for it. I think by the time they got to their middle teens they had probably had enough of shops, having been in them since about the age of eight. So did they ever want to come into it? Not really! Nicola left school at a time when I had some underwear shops called 'In the Pink'. I had five altogether, including one in Leeds, which I suggested Nicola managed. It was a small shop in a safe environment, so she tried that for twelve months but then when Sonya left school, that's when they got together on the beauty business. They're great girls and I'd like to give them the chance to speak for themselves.

Sonya says: 'Dad is quite remarkable. It's funny because your dad's just your dad and sometimes you take him for granted, but then every now and then you have to pinch yourself and think what he's done in building up this huge business. I know he's my dad, but I honestly believe he's special. Even though Poundworld is so big, he is still so hands-on. He's definitely different, but I think one of the great things about my dad is that he hasn't changed over the years. The energy and the youthful attitude is just the same as it's always been.'

'I can remember the market days. He was working very hard, yet I've got a lot of memories of him at home as well so it seemed to balance,' adds Nicola. 'I don't quite know how he managed, but he did. We spent a lot of time going off with him to work. Dad likes to involve the whole family as much as possible.'

Sonya says: 'I only have vague memories of the first shop in Wakefield, but quite clear recollections of the big three-floor store in Bradford, where my grandma used to run the café. It was a big part of our childhood, going over to Bradford on a Saturday and in the school holidays with Dad. He certainly made sure we were thrown in at the deep end. My sister and I would be given boxes to stand on to bring us up to the customers' level. I think I would have been about seven years old when I had the responsibility of using the till! My sister used to work on the front till and I would be at the back.

'It hardly seems possible now that Dad was running his nightclubs at night, his shops during the day and still managing to spend time at home with us, but he did. He seemed perfectly able to do it all. On Christmas Day he would come in from the clubs at two or three o'clock in the morning and then still manage to be up, bright-eyed, for the present opening. I don't think he's a sleeper, just a power napper.

'My sister Nicola is three years older than me. She left school first and went to work for my dad – I didn't get involved until much later. I left school when I was sixteen and both Nicola and I wanted to get into the health and fitness business so we joined forces. She had been working for Dad for a couple of years and we decided to go off to college together. We did our training and then worked for a little time afterwards to gain some experience. The plan was always to open somewhere of our own. I'd got *an image of a salon in my head, which was maybe a little place on the side of the road, but we ended up stumbling across an old converted watermill in Newmillerdam!*

'It was a pub that had closed down. We found it, and although it was much bigger than the places we had originally thought of, we could see it had great potential. Dad had faith in us. He knew we'd had the right grounding and he backed us from the start – I think business must be in the genes. I was eighteen and my sister was twenty-one and it was quite a challenge. We literally opened the doors on day one and we worked all hours we could to make it work. Gradually, it became a thriving business.

'It was hard work but we loved it. We ran it very successfully for twelve years until our children started to arrive. It just became the right time to get out. It wasn't an easy decision, but it was the right one for us. Customers still come up and say they wish that we were still in the business, but we both think that we made the right call at the right time.

'Obviously, it was all made possible by my dad and it was a great experience. Dad encouraged us a great deal. I think maybe he had a dream of us all going into the family business but he brought us up to be quite independently minded, so when we said we wanted to do something different, he realised he wouldn't be able to take us off our chosen paths. I know he looks back and is proud of us.

'He never once said: "Don't you think you should

start with something smaller?" It was a big project. He would pop in to see us most Saturdays, but he let us get on with it our way. I'm sure if we'd been sitting there with no clients he would have been asking what had gone wrong, but because things went pretty well, he left us to it but we knew he was always there if we needed him. But then the children came along and they were more important than the business. Dad agreed at the time – he is very straightforward and decisive about business.

'Of course when it comes to making money, my brother Christopher is more like my dad than Nicola or me. I remember he was already thinking about earning money from a very early age. My grandad used to take him to the cash and carry to go and buy sweets. Christopher would go along and choose the sweets he wanted, then bring them back and lay them all out on his little trolley, ready to sell to any friends who came round! There are seven years between my brother and I, but when it came to making money, he grew up very quickly. He sold the penny sweets for two pence! Christopher started to follow Dad very early on, obviously. I think he was definitely born with that same money making gene.

'It certainly wasn't all business for us when we were growing up. Dad always found time for family outings; in fact, he loved them. Some people imagine family life might have suffered because of Dad's passion for his work but no, I don't feel my dad was missing at all and he's no different with the *grandchildren. He just loves being with the family. A large part of my childhood was spent in the Lake District with my dad. We would go on a Saturday once the shops had closed and stay overnight on our boat. My brother and I loved it. My sister, being a little older, was often spending time at home with friends. We had some great times and have some wonderful memories of spending time with Dad.'*

Nicola says: 'As children, we were fortunate enough to go abroad from an early age. It is only now that I have a family of my own that I realise just how hard Dad must have worked to make everything possible for us.'

Sonya adds: 'It blows your mind how much Poundworld has expanded recently. The great thing is that Dad's not any different from how he's always been; he's still got that fire in his belly. I think that comes from where he started and it's never left him. We're reminded of it in a good way; he never wants us to forget where we come from. Dad has always kept our feet very firmly on the ground. He was strict when we were growing up, even well past an age when dads are meant to be strict! He's still strict now, in a nice way. He likes everything to be just so. He's a perfectionist, really, in everything, not just in business.

'His values are the same as Grandad's. The tradition in the family is very strong. It comes from my grandad and grandma. They were remarkable for the hours they worked and the determination they had. My grandma is still working hard now! Dad

just knew from a very young age that he wanted to take it to a different level. As soon as he had Nicola, he wanted a better life for his kids. Even today, everything he does is for us.

'*Dad is very warm and sensitive. He can get emotional about children or his past and where he's come from. He must have an unbelievable sense of achievement. He had no inherited money to help him along the way, just unswerving energy, and he put in endless hard work. My dad looks young and he dresses young; he's like Peter Pan in that he never seems to change. He always looked younger than other people's dads when I was at school and he has a very young outlook on life.*

'*We didn't have much involvement in the clubs as we were so young at the time. Of course we did go sometimes. There were some massive events at Dollars and who could forget singing and dancing with The Three Degrees? As we grew up and it came to socialising, we went off in a different direction. Then Dad was very protective. He was always there to pick us up; he left his nightclub to drive to pick us up and drop us off at home and then he would get back in the car and go back to work. He never wanted us coming home in taxis. Somehow he managed to juggle that with work. My friends all thought I was so lucky, but I was mortified when he kept turning up to pick me up.*

'*Nicola and I are now distanced a little bit from the business because it has grown so much. The buildings got bigger and bigger and there are more and more staff. We don't know everybody anymore but Dad is still sitting at this desk in charge of it all. He has hardly changed at all. His hands-on approach is still amazing.*

'Of course it's different now my dad and my brother Christopher know they have each other. They are good at different things, but they are really very similar. Sometimes they clash and neither will back down so you don't want to be caught in the middle! It's that passion that they share that drives them both on.

'Dad is a very humble person and he instilled that quality in all of us. Whether we have the best of everything, nobody would ever know. He always wanted us to keep our feet firmly on the ground and nothing was taken for granted. You knew how hard it was to earn the money, and you knew it was important to be very careful with money.

'He is still scared of being skint. "You never know," is what he's always said. He can never relax and now when he's not thinking about himself or us, he's thinking about his grandchildren! He's looked after one generation and then another and now he's onto the third. If he could carry on, he would do to the next, and the next and the next.'

Nicola says: 'His friends are all old friends from football. He hasn't changed; he has never lost sight of where he's come from. He is quite youthful, although age is his only bugbear. I think he wants to go on forever. I just wish my grandad could have been around to see Poundworld's success. He was such an important person to my Dad. He was successful anyway, but I can't imagine what he'd make of all this.

'I've always been very proud of Dad. When I was at school, lots of the other girls used to fancy him. The standing joke in the family now is that he has the look of Dustin Hoffman and I think he has been mistaken a couple of times!

'I think he's a night owl, really. Those two-week beach holidays probably drove him crazy because he likes to be doing something all the time. He would do it because he knew as a family that's what we all wanted and he would love playing in the pool. I know it was hard for him to switch off. He's not a "sit-still" type of person. His energy is amazing.

'When we were little we never realised that often times were difficult. We never felt he was struggling; it was just his way of life. It was just what he did. I know he worries about being retired. He doesn't like the word or the acceptance that you're getting older as well; I think he will always do something. I don't think he would ever want to retire.

'We have always been made to see that you should always be doing something and striving to do something, and not sitting back at home. As children, we never got punished – he only had to look at you! We didn't do it in the first place. We did push the boundaries in our teenage years, I suppose, but there *was always respect there. He was strict in that he always wanted to stop you making mistakes. He always used to say he could "see round that corner". He used to vet boyfriends, so in some ways it's amazing we're married – he still vets the husbands sometimes!*

'*We were so pleased for Dad when the business was successful. We both went to college and worked at times for other people. Dad's ethos is "You don't work for anyone else". When we had the beauty business, we worked really hard because we desperately didn't want to let him down. He put faith as well as money into the business and we wanted to succeed for him.*

'*Working is a big thing for Dad. We always had to work when we were at school, in holidays and on Saturdays, in shops because Dad drove us over to the Bradford shop and put us in a position on a till or whatever, but we weren't just stacking shelves, we had responsible jobs too. I loved it when Dad was based there. It was quite big, a little home from home there. I did a lot of growing up there, and it gave us good grounding as to what it means to work. He's passed on the same thing to us.*'

'*Dad was always competitive when it came to sports day at school...*' *she adds. Both sisters chorus,* '*No prizes for second!*' *Nicola explains that was her father's attitude to competition. She says:* '*From being little, I remember he always won the dads' race. We'd have to come home with every cup from every race otherwise we hadn't done well. We'd have pictures with Dad with his cup, and me and Sonya with our cups. Fortunately, we were quite sporty so there were quite a few red ribbons. We all had to win. He wasn't interested in the taking part; he was warming us up beforehand and behaving very competitively. Even Christopher was limbered up when he was three years old!*

'We had a great upbringing. Because I was the oldest, Dad had still got family on the fairground and when I finished my exams at sixteen, I went to stay for two weeks with some relations. I had an absolute ball! I was supposed to come back for a week and I begged to go back and did it a couple of times, and I got a link then with my generation of relatives on the fairgrounds that I still keep in touch with. I lived in a wagon and it was great fun. We had a great social life. Just walking round the fairground and the buzz of it all was brilliant!

'Dad instinctively shies away from the limelight, but over the years he has learned to handle it. I remember he once said to me that when we were at senior school we had more confidence than him. Now he has become much more confident although he found it difficult doing Sonya's wedding speech; he was shaking.'

Sonya explains: 'I got married first and Dad did my wedding speech and he was very nervous, so when Nicola got married, she didn't have speeches so Dad could relax. He was very emotional, especially talking about his children. I think he would be fine now, especially after all his experience in front of the television cameras.'

CHAPTER TWELVE

LIKE FATHER, LIKE SON

You think you're as old as the hills when you're twenty-one, but years later, you realise you're not as wise and grown-up as you once thought you were. Until I was twenty-one, I mainly did as I was told, though I used to challenge my dad on a daily basis all the way through my teens. He never took as much notice of my ideas as I thought he should have done. All he kept saying was: 'When it's your turn, then you'll do what you want. While you're working with me, you'll do as I tell you.' For me that was very frustrating and later on, I decided that I was never going to hold back my own son in the same way. I wanted to repeat some of my dad's excellent disciplines, but I didn't want to frustrate my son in the way I myself had felt frustrated.

I'm talking about when I was fourteen to eighteen years old. When my son left high school, I said: 'If you don't watch it, you'll do what your dad did and your teens will be gone and your twenties will be gone, and you'll wake up some time in your mid-thirties and think, "Where's all that gone?"' He's thirty-two now and he's said exactly that to me. He is trying to find his way to stop doing what we're doing in such a frustrating way. I said to him: 'You can't, it's in your DNA. You're fighting something that is so ingrained in you that you can't help yourself.'

My work ethic is not motivated by greed because I honestly don't think I'm a greedy person. It is because I am constantly looking for a better lifestyle, constantly looking at doing all the things that I think I should do; I am motivated by achievement. That is me and I suppose he is exactly the same.

In the past there have been times when I've said to Lorraine: 'That son of yours is getting on my ******* nerves.' She looks at me and says: 'Now you know why we are not together.' It is that single-mindedness that sets us apart, I suppose. I take every challenge in business head-on and put everything I have into this job. It's no different to being a dedicated sportsman. No one can imagine how much time the best sportsman puts into working on being as good as possible, whether it's a runner or a cyclist, or whatever. They'll get up at four o'clock in the morning and run before they go to work. I look at business in a very similar way to that. They just want to be good at what they do, and so do I.

My son Christopher always has plenty to say for himself and he's become an integral part of Poundworld so it's clearly time I let him speak for himself.

Christopher says: 'I have always been fascinated by my dad's business as far back as I can remember. My interest probably began when I was four or five years old, just starting at school. I used to go visiting shops with my dad all the time – it just seemed like the most amazing world. From as long ago as I can remember, I used to like it. But he didn't make me do it, unless of course he was secretly brainwashing me! I'm joking, of course. I genuinely loved it and I always thought it was 100 per cent my choice. I enjoyed going with him and working on the shop floors. We only had a handful of shops back then and they were all pretty local, in Wakefield, Bradford and Barnsley. I spent a lot of time in the Bradford store, which was one of his main shops. When I was young, from about the age of ten, I worked there every Saturday. I really liked the Bradford shop because it was large and usually very busy, and particularly because my grandma used to have the café there.

'I must have been small because I can remember standing on a box to operate the till. I worked in the toy department, and as a kid I used to love it. There was a talking parrot that cost £19.99, and things like that. I spent a lot of time in Bradford; I was there pretty much every week until I was fourteen. When we opened a shop in Leeds city centre, I used to demonstrate toys. Then I realised I was working for free!

'I don't think I got pocket money, but I think I was pretty well looked after. I just loved selling

things. I used to do car boot sales with my grandma – I think they started when I was about fourteen. My grandad had just passed away and my grandma was at a loose end so we sort of went into "partnership" with each other. I asked my dad if I could buy stock from him. He agreed, so I used to go into the shop in Wakefield and ask the manager what sold. I then went into the warehouse and chose merchandise and bought on a weekly basis. Dad used to come and see my grandma and me every week at the car boot sales. We used to sell our carload out really quickly and then he would bring us extra stock. We paid for the stock, but fortunately, the delivery was free. Thank goodness!

'My dad used to turn up at about 10 o'clock just as my supplies of stock were diminishing and he would hang around for a little bit. I recall he was impressed with the way we had everything laid out and displayed as attractively as possible. He used to say: "Why can't our shops be as clean and smart as this stall?" That continued for a year or so and then my grandma invested in a trailer so we could take more stock ourselves – I really hit the big time then!

'I just loved getting involved in all aspects of the business. I used to do a sweet shop in the kids' disco in one of the nightclubs. When I was thirteen or fourteen, there was Kikos in Pontefract, though it seemed they changed names a few times. I was up for lots of different enterprises; I loved the idea of making money. Another time, Grandma used to pick

me up from school at four o'clock and we would race to Bradford and set up my sweet shop.

'I think the approach to hard work and the ability to sell to the public must be hereditary. It seems to go way back in the family. I can see now that it might seem a little unusual, but if you look at our family background, it is perfectly natural. The other thing about our family is that we stick together. My dad has always supported me in everything I've wanted to do. I know there are a lot of father-son business relationships that are difficult and there are situations when the son can perhaps be in his forties or fifties and still can't do what he wants to do in the company. But in our business, working for my dad, even if we don't always see eye to eye on everything, we always get on. To be frank, I don't feel I am working *for* my dad, but with *my dad. There is a big difference, I believe. He has always been a massive support.*

'The timing of my arrival in the business seems to have been right. I have two older sisters and I know he tried to get them involved. One sister worked in a shop and she hated it. I was different: put me in a shop and I love it! We're just different. I never wanted to do anything else. I never wanted to go to university or travel, or anything; I was adamant. I left school, finished my last exam when I was sixteen. I ran out of that school for the last time and I felt "YES!" I was so pleased it was over; I couldn't stand being in that classroom. I was desperate to get out and get into the business.

'Getting a taste for retail with my grandma and then my dad for years, the older I got, the more I found myself itching to get going. I did the markets because that satisfied a certain need. In lessons, I used to be writing down plans for work. I used to have the kids' disco. My dad recently found a flyer for the kids' disco; it brought back a lot of happy memories. In Wakefield, my dad had a Bargain Centre shop and on the top floor was this big space, which was a toyshop for a while. I used to work there but it didn't last too long. Toys really only sell well at Christmas so Dad closed the toyshop; it was left empty. Then I think it was his idea to open it up again as a kids' play area. He got a bouncy castle to get kids up there. The floor space was massive and all the toys were right at the back. It was 50p to go on the bouncy castle for a kid to play on and obviously that brought people upstairs to look at the toys.

'Dad said to me: "You can have it, if you want." I think he wanted it to pay its way and he didn't want to have to pay staff, so if I did it, then it would be free! I used to go and sit there on a Saturday with a little table, taking 50p from each kid. And Dad let me keep the money! I must have been really young then, like about twelve or thirteen. I think I always worked on a Saturday, either demonstrating toys or working on this bouncy castle. I used to throw a lot of "sickies" because I just hated school that much. I would be sitting there, studying algebra, thinking,

"This is a waste of my time. I don't want to bother any more with this."

'Often when I was at home my grandad would ring me up and say: "You're not ill, are you?" I'd admit straight away that I was feeling fine. "Right," he'd say, "I'll pick you up in ten minutes! You can come with me and do some work." The majority of times I thought, "Good." He used to pick me up and take me to one of my dad's nightclubs, where he would empty the slot machines and then service them. I used to help him do that instead of sitting in a classroom. Then we would stop for lunch and have fish and chips or something. I would count all the pound coins and it seemed like a fun day out.

'I would go to the bank with him and then we went to the cash 'n' carry, because my grandad used to get all the stock for my grandma's café. I must have been very young because I sat on the end of his trolley. It was amazing and I was astonished to see how cheap sweets were. That's when I ended up buying some drinks and sweets to have with the bouncy castle. I was sitting there all day and the kids were coming off, hot and thirsty, so they wanted a drink and a sweet. I don't think I asked my dad – I just did it, put a few drinks on for the kids. My dad was happy; he said: "No problem." So my grandad used to get them from the cash 'n' carry for me and I would sell them on this little table next to the bouncy castle.

'That led to turning the whole floor into a kids' play area. I can't remember if it was my dad's idea *or mine.* [Chris says: 'It was actually Christopher's idea, the last thing I wanted to get involved with was bouncy castles and lots of lively children!'] *Anyway, Dad helped fund it and I can't remember if I paid him back or not – I'm not really sure. I remember I paid some money back later on. But for quite a while I had a kids' play area up there, with my dad supporting me. That went on for about three years. So I did a kids' disco on a Friday, play area on a Saturday, and the market on a Sunday. I used to go into school on a Monday morning absolutely knackered.*

'*Midweek, I would have to go to cash 'n' carries to get the stock. My grandma used to take me to Bradford one night of the week to go to the cash 'n' carry. She would take me to another cash 'n' carry in Leeds on another night. And the other two nights, we used to go to the warehouse to get stock. So that was four nights a week, and Friday was back to the disco. I was working every day of the week. On Saturday night, I used to load the trailer up ready for the morning car boot sale. I would get back in the middle of the afternoon dead beat! Then I would be back in school, feeling exhausted. The teachers would be saying: "Where's your homework?" And I would have to admit: "I haven't done it."*

'*It's hard for me to put my finger on exactly what my motivation was and always has been. It's not the money; it's just the enjoyment I get from the work. Dad always says the same. It's the pleasure and satisfaction of working and making something work.*

I want to do things as well as I can. Even with the kids' play area, I tried to make it as good as possible. There was a stockroom next door that we never used, so I turned it into a Santa's Grotto at Christmas. I had two or three days off school and painted it, fitted it all out. I don't think I made any money; it was just something I wanted to do; it was creative. I was a little young to play Santa Claus myself at fourteen years old, so I interviewed other people for the job. I enjoyed it. I had elves all around the grotto and the little kids loved it.

'The play area was called Jungle Jim's. In the morning before I went to school I used to have to make all the sandwiches and everything, then my grandma would take them on trays during the day and I used to have to sprint from school. It was a ten-minute run with my satchel as the party ran from 4pm until 6pm, so I used to have to get someone from my dad's shop to go upstairs and look after it for about five minutes to get it going. I finished school at four and I would run and get there just past four, with my school uniform still on. I would stay until six. Then Dad used to pick me up. With the Jungle Jim's and the kids' disco and the market, Dad didn't really have to come and drop stock off on a Sunday car boot. It wasn't really very cost-effective, but at the time he was doing it for the greater good, or for me, wasn't he?

'Grandma is as sharp as anything. We have always been close but when my grandad died, we became

like partners in crime. Before then I spent a lot of time with Grandad because he used to be working a lot. I used to go on day trips with my grandparents. My mum used to work at my sisters' beauty salon so I was at a loose end night times when I was young. After I got back from the cash 'n' carry, I would often go to my grandparents' house for tea a few nights a week. We were all really close. We are still close now because my grandma comes in every day, but that's a bit different. I try to have ten minutes with her as she makes tea and toast every morning, but I am really busy here. This job is very full-on all the time.

'*When I was growing up I was always quite ambitious and wanted to earn money. My dad could have said, "No, you're not doing that," but most times he let me do whatever I wanted to try. I used to take stuff into school to sell; I would buy stock from my dad at the warehouse. I used to spend a lot of time in the warehouse – I loved walking round there and looking at what was going on sale. I was fascinated by it. I used to know all the staff in there on first-name terms. The first warehouse I knew of was a stockroom above the shop in Bradford. Then we had a much bigger warehouse at Ouzlewell Green. Sometimes it felt as though I lived in that warehouse. That was 10,000 square feet, which at the time seemed huge, but now we've got a store that is that big. I remember Dad's office used to have palm tree wallpaper – it was straight out of Del Boy's stylebook!*

'In the warehouse I can remember one day finding this box of electric scissors. Battery-operated, they were long forgotten and covered in dust. I don't think they were selling. I showed them to my dad and said: "I've just found these in the warehouse. Can I buy 'em?" "Just take them," he told me. They had obviously been sitting there for years. I got a couple of boxes and took them to school. They turned out to be surprisingly popular and created quite a craze at the school. They were quite fun! Lots of kids bought some and eventually I got into trouble because kids were cutting up everything. I did get in trouble with the teachers a few times for things like that.

'Somebody asked my dad if he wanted to go to the Far East, where much of our stock was imported from by wholesalers. He agreed to go and asked me if I wanted to come with him. Obviously, I jumped at the chance because I was thrilled by the idea. He rang the school and asked if I could have the time off to go on the trip. They said: "No, his education is more important." But my dad is not used to taking no for an answer so he replied that this trip was very much an important part of my education and I was going anyway. He just said: "I'm taking him, so you can do what you want."

'That's how it all really started for me, with my first trip to China when I was fifteen. It turned out to be a really crucial time for the business: it was the start of the imports, which have helped to revolutionise the business. At that time my dad used to sell some *imports, but not many. I think he took me with him to help me get my feet under the table. It certainly worked. I was even more fascinated by the business and that interest built up until I left school when I was sixteen. Then I took a pay cut and did some real work on the markets.*

'When I left school and started work it was a very exciting time for me, but it was hardly a conventional beginning. On day one I arrived and said to Dad: "What do you want me to do?" He just looked at me and said: "I don't know. Find something!" I still don't know if that was his way of challenging me, or whether he really didn't know what I should be doing. He'd never really delegated like that before; he had always done everything himself, so when I left school and asked where he wanted me to start, I genuinely don't think he knew! For a year I spent a lot of time observing, just looking at what went on and who did what. It was a great learning process. Then I started in a bigger way when I was seventeen or eighteen.

'That first trip to the Far East took me a long way out of my comfort zone. I was always a quiet lad when I was younger, I wasn't particularly confident or outgoing, and there I was, in a foreign country with a big group of grown men. There were a lot of people Dad knew over there and had to meet with and in the evenings they would be going out for meals and drinks. I'm sure Dad sometimes felt uncomfortable when he realised he had his fifteen-

year-old son sitting at the table with him. The men would be talking about all sorts of adult things. There was a lot of very adult swearing and all that sort of thing.

'I was always itching to be in the business. I don't think Dad ever pushed me to say I wanted to join him – I think he let me make my own mind up – and from an early age, I have always loved the business. I loved being with my dad, choosing merchandise, visiting warehouses, opening shops; I loved the retail world. It's not just one thing about our business I love; it's a combination of everything. It changes and evolves over the years and there are so many different things I enjoy about it.

'Today, what I like best is finding a product in, say, China; buying that product, developing it, creating the artwork and everything, and then bringing that product to market and getting it on the shelves and seeing someone buy it. It's brilliant! I was at a shop opening the other day in Leicester and I saw these products like that coming through the till. It's taken six months to get them to the shops and to see them going through the till is fantastic. I like to see a busy shop; it gives me a lot of satisfaction. I think it's quite a creative business. I wouldn't like to say I'm creative in any other areas other than buying stock and selling. People always say to me: "Did you always have this plan in mind?" It's always the same question and I really don't know the answer. It seems like it just happened; in a way it was planned.

'I think I came along at the right time. I was probably about sixteen and just before I left school and got involved, Dad said to me: "Look, I've got the nightclubs and I've got the shops. I'll be honest with you: I'm a bit pissed off with the shops. What do you want to do?" I just said: "One hundred per cent the shops." I like going out to nightclubs but I wouldn't want to run one, though funnily enough I've just bought a pub. Dad was very good and gave me the option. I think he was pleased because a lot of competition opened up in the retail world at that time.

'Supermarkets became more aggressive – there was the emergence of Poundstretcher, Poundland and all these other companies. I think he was steering away from the shops a little. He was, by his own admission, a bit tired. I was eager to go on with them. Fortunately, he said: "Fine, I'll carry on with the shops." He could have said he was fed up and weary with retail, he could have been selfish and done what he wanted to do, but instead he said, "OK, let's do it then!" and we cracked on.

'This was just as I was going through my GCSE exams. Mark Ward, who came with us on the trip to New York, started here. He had about a six-month start on me, but I got involved just as soon as I could. I was desperate to get going. In between my GCSEs, either my mum or my dad would drop me off at a store to merchandise it (that means to put the stock on the shelves). I love to design the layout and organise everything (Mark wasn't really that experienced in *that area). I thoroughly enjoyed myself, but it was a baptism of fire.*

'I learned that skill from going to car boots and working with Dad over the years. I learned an awful lot from him, of course. I really enjoyed setting out our goods for sale. It felt good, and it felt natural; it has always been important to me. I think the first couple I tried, I didn't always get it right. It took a little time to learn. I used to mirror what my dad did and it just kind of evolved. It was something I loved to do, and something I believe I am good at. Since then of course it has evolved a lot more. Now we have space plans and detailed designs of how we want the shop to look. Of course it varies according to the size and shape of shop and it is becoming more complex. Initially, all I tried to do was fairly approximate; a plan on the back of a fag packet, you might say. I would look at sales per space. It was just roughly what we had in the warehouse went into the shops; it was thought out a little bit.

'While I was doing my GCSEs I merchandised quite a few shops. When I left school, it became pretty much my job then. Mark Ward and I became a good team. When there was a shop opening, he used to interview the staff and I used to merchandise the shops and we would get ready for opening. That went on for a couple of years. In between shop openings, I didn't really know what else I was supposed to be doing. That's when I started looking at the business for errors we were making.

I remember I had a conversation with my dad when I was about seventeen, I think, and I said I had just been looking at the purchasing and learned a lot about our mistakes!

'With the confidence of youth, I suppose, I said to my dad: "Look, you're buying a 10-pack of hairgrips at 40p, and Laurie is buying a 5-pack of hairgrips at 55p." I could see there was conflict in what we were buying. I said: "Do you mind if I look after the buying because I think I can do it?" It sounds pushy now, and it didn't happen overnight, but I had always been so interested in the business. My dad used to take me to UK trade shows when I was younger – to places like the NEC, near Birmingham. I don't think he insisted I went; I wanted to go out of curiosity and particularly when we used to buy toys. They were my forte. I was a kid and I knew what was current, and my dad didn't have a clue! When we looked through toys, I knew what was in and what was out. Toys go in and out of fashion, like lots of other things – you need a younger mind.*

'I'm thirty-two now and I don't know where the time has gone, to be honest. I just know I wouldn't have missed it for the world! There were three big things I did. The first thing I managed to persuade Dad to do was the rebranding, because I wanted to rename the shops Poundworld in 2002. I remember the conversation we had quite clearly; some things stick in my mind. When I said: "Look, I've been thinking about this, can we rebrand?" Dad's first* response was his familiar retort to every suggestion: "How much is it going to cost?"

'That would be the response every time I came up with something I wanted to change or introduce. He would question it. It would be: "Why do you want to do that?" and "How much is it going to cost?" I tried to explain that I believed "Everything's £1" was a bit dull. He said: "Well, what do you want to call it?" Obviously, I'd been scribbling ideas for a new title down on my notepads for ages and I liked the idea of Poundworld. He was cautious and said: "Right..." I explained that if we opened up a new shop it was not going to cost any more to set it up with the new name. Just the graphics would change; everything else would be the same. He argued then that we would have different shops with different brands. I said: "Yes, but if we start as we mean to go on then eventually we'll have Poundworld all over the place." Fortunately, that is exactly how it has turned out.

'The first Poundworld was a shop we opened in Salford in 2003. The second thing I introduced was a much-improved process of shop fitting a little later. When I first used to merchandise the shops we would buy second-hand shelving and I used to cut my hands to shreds, trying to bang the shelves in. It was horrible, absolutely horrible! We'd get dirty shelves and spend ages cleaning them and banging them in. There was no flexibility. We were spending minimal amounts on the shopfit; we left the floors as *they were, and the ceilings as they were. So I said to Dad: "Can we spend a bit more money on the shopfit, because they are pretty crap?" I could see Poundland and what they were doing. They had about forty or fifty shops at the time and I could see where they were going. They were importing from China and we weren't; their shopfits were well done and ours weren't. Of course when I suggested improving the shopfits, it was: "How much is that going to cost?" Eventually, I persuaded him to it.*

'The third thing was the EPOS [electronic point of sale] *system and that was the hardest. At first, I didn't fully understand it myself, but when I started doing the buying, I knew we needed to improve our stock control. With EPOS, all the figures are right there on your computer. I think my dad's stock control was shouting to my Uncle Laurie in the warehouse and asking how many cases we had left of whatever item! In the Ouzlewell Green office his office door opened directly onto the warehouse and he used to open it and yell: "Laurie, Laurie!"*

'EPOS was a big step forward. It seems obvious now that we needed it, but it was not easy to convince my dad. This was introduced in 2002. Dad goes with everything eventually, but this took a bit more persuasion. When I first started doing the buying, the lack of technology was crippling. I used to have to go to the warehouse and count how many cartons of whatever we had and then work out how many had gone out and how many we needed to order.

I remember telling Dad EPOS would cost about £250,000, which at the time seemed ridiculously expensive. Then we were barely showing that as a profit.

'My dad said: "Not a chance!" First of all, he didn't understand it, but he said moneywise, we just couldn't afford it. Not a chance! Mark Ward and I then worked it back to try to show the cost in different ways. We worked out the cost per shop per year. Dad said: "No." Then we tried per shop per month. He said: "No." Per shop per week? "No." Per shop per day? "No." When we got it down to per shop per hour, it was only like 10p an hour per shop. "That seems all right," he went. He agreed, but it was expensive for us and I used to get a lot of stick over that, for years. Now, of course, it is impossible to imagine doing what we do without it.

'We are just now revamping the system. I think in the end the system we bought was about £200,000, which served its purpose, and we have developed it over the years to help us get where we need to be, but it is still outdated. What we are moving to now is a £2 million system so it's a bit scary. But you couldn't run the business now without the system. It has grown so much; it would be impossible.

'Part of my argument for rebranding was inspired by an incident when I heard a woman tell her husband that she would not go into one of our shops. At that time I had become obsessed by Poundland, absolutely obsessed with them, because I could see what they

were achieving: their shops were smarter than ours and their prices were sharper. Take pocket tissues, for example. We used to sell a 10-pack bought from a UK importer for £1. They would do a 24-pack they had imported from China for £1. Everything we did, we just couldn't compete and yet I knew we needed to be able to compete.

'When it came to trying to get new units, I said: "We're not opening shops up quickly enough, we're only doing a couple a month at the moment; it's not enough." Dad said: "We're trying, but we can't get them. The landlords just say: 'We don't want you.'" I said: "They don't want us because we look like an independent. We need to have a corporate-looking brand." Over the course of six months or a year it might have taken me, different things were adding up in his head. I kept saying: "Let's change."

'The incident that convinced me we had to change happened outside our shop in Wakefield. I saw a middle-aged couple shopping. The guy stopped and said to the lady: "Let's go in here," but she looked down her nose and said: "Oh, I'm not going in there!" It was our shop and I could see it didn't look very smart but I knew that was because of what they could afford in the shopfit. I had just left school; I was sixteen. It was 2003 when we did the first one. I'm thirty-two now – I suppose I have packed a lot in, a lot of work, that is.

'It's mad because I've just done it for so long. When I first started doing the buying, suppliers used

to come and see me. Up until then, Dad had always done it. I was sick of hearing: "Your dad used to do it this way." I'd say: "Well, he might have done but now I'm doing the buying." They were always really patronising. I never used to wear a smart shirt; even now I'm pretty casual – I would come in with trainers and jeans and a T-shirt. The sellers would start by wanting to see "Chris" and then the confusion would really start. There would be a "Which Chris?" conversation. Dad realised what it was going to be like when I left school, that's why I became Chris junior and he became Chris senior, or sometimes he was Chris and I was Christopher, but that was still open to confusion. I suppose in any family business you are in the shadow so it was understandable, but we do seem to have a brilliant balance between us nowadays.

'The good thing is that my dad knows that although we clash on some things, when it comes to the buying and merchandising, he lets me get on with it because I couldn't cope otherwise. He trusts me to do that. They are really smart shops and I feel we are getting there but it is a never-ending task. Retail is detail, and I think it goes on forever; you can always up your game. I find it fascinating.

'I love what I do; I love it. It's a bit of a different era now because going back historically, it was quite easy to grow turnover in a store. We have had the rebranding and had to spend more money on the shopfits – you get more people through the door, you

get more brand awareness, you create more footfall, you start buying brands... My dad never used to buy brands. He refused because there was almost no margin in it; the profit involved was tiny. But obviously once again I was obsessed with Poundland and I could see what they were doing, and they were doing brands.

'I persuaded Dad to start putting some brands in our shops – it does impress people to see Heinz beans and stuff. Brands nowadays are two-thirds of our business, before it was literally nothing. It wasn't there to drive footfall into the store. Stuff like well-known brands of toothpaste are vital, basic lines like that bring people in. Dad is always a little reluctant at first and he eventually comes round.

'The good thing with my dad though is that it hasn't been a difficult battle. That initial resistance is always there but he is always prepared to listen, and if I put up a good argument and get my facts right, he usually agrees in the end. Of course what he did when he was younger was just as vital. We have said to each other, I wouldn't be where I am if it wasn't for him, and vice versa. Because obviously, I had a great starting point: there is no way if I was not my father's son I would be here today. All those years he spent with market stalls and with his first few shops laid the groundwork for everything that followed. If he hadn't started it all, I don't know where I would be today. It was a different time and a different generation, and what he achieved was amazing.

'We do have similar energy levels – it is pretty frightening how alike we are in that way. I don't sleep an awful lot, like my dad. And where we are very similar is the way we both wake in the night in sweats. That doesn't happen as much now because the business is a little more stable. There were times when the next day we both said: "Oh God, I woke up absolutely drenched in sweat." It is so bad there is like a puddle in the bed and I've got to get out. Neither my dad nor I are exactly sure what it is, just an unconscious concern that results in a very bad night's sleep, anxiety that comes out during the day.

'Three or four years ago, when I was still in my twenties, that was definitely the worst time; I often used to wake up wet. I would talk to my dad about it and he said it had been exactly the same with him. Sometimes it turned out that it was happening on the same night, perhaps when something particularly stressful was going on. It shows how similar we are. Definitely, my mentality has come from my dad because that's been ingrained for years and generations past. I say it's in my blood, I think the shop floor is in my blood; the mentality, I think. There's a real code of behaviour – you do this, you don't do that – the basic principles of work ethics and drive are laid down. Dad has been dedicated for so long it's amazing; he's relentless.

'I'm not sure I will have that same energy and will to succeed at that age. We'll see. He did warn me that my twenties would be over before I knew *it and he was right. Even when I was eighteen or nineteen, I remember my girlfriend at the time was pissed off because I used to get up early on a Saturday morning and say: "I'm sorry, I'm going to Harrogate." I would get the bus to Harrogate and work in our shop. We didn't have area managers or regional managers, so when we had fifteen or eighteen shops Mark Ward and I were in theory the area managers of those shops. During that period when I was seventeen or eighteen, I moved out of area management and into buying.*

'Our initial target for shops was fifty; then we said 100, just choosing a round number. It kind of becomes where the business takes over a little bit and you need to be bigger. To get the buying power, you need to open more shops. We always looked at Poundland and we knew we needed to graduate to buying in volume so we needed more shops to create the buying power. Then you've always got to beat your figures from previous years to get the bank's support. There is a sort of spiral where you always have to beat your figures from the previous year and you can't do that without expanding and without EPOS.

'A nine-to-five guy wouldn't be able to do this job, certainly not from scratch. You would have to be like Poundland – a very corporate structure, and they have more than 60 people in their buying team and are only twice the size. We have five – well, I suppose with assistants, I've got seven. Getting

on with people is so important. My dad loves that aspect of the business and so do I. That's what I love about the car boots and the markets, and spending so much time in the office now; that's what I miss. When I was in Leicester the other day, I was on the till. I was helping out and just bagging stuff up and chatting to customers. I was just getting that feeling for when we had the new till system fitted so I was keeping my eyes on that before we roll it out. I enjoyed very much listening to what people were saying. On the market definitely my dad used to see and hear and pick up a lot – I'm sure that's where he learned such a lot.

'I don't think Dad or me would ever want to stand up on a box and deliver a load of spiel. We are both very similar in that we are a bit more reserved. I think the products speak for themselves and that is the way we make up for not having that loud "Roll up, roll up, get your whatever today!"-type personalities and put it instead in signs and what we call "flash".

'A lot of people ask me how we sell such bargains as top-quality toothpaste for £1 when it's £3 elsewhere. The long and short of it is that supermarkets rip people off. The so-called "supermarket price wars" was bollocks – I don't know where it is. They might battle a little on fresh food, like milk and things like eggs and bread, but in terms of other items, the idea of a price war is a myth. They put up this big façade of "Tesco drops 5,000 items in price". I'd like to see that in writing and be allowed to check on where

they have actually dropped their prices. We are selling stuff at £1 that is £1.50 or £1.80 in supermarkets.

'The most-repeated comment by a mile from customers is: "I only came in for a couple of bits and I've got a basketful." We are learning more about customer shopping habits and where to place products and how "eye level is buy level" and the benefits of promotion bays. There are things we do knowing at key seasons what sells. It could be as simple as at Christmas when on a side promotion table we put Blu-Tack, drawing pins, Sellotape... You are steering the customer towards certain things. It is becoming more scientific all the time. It is interesting in a different way, but I do miss being on the shop floors; I'm sure Dad does as well. It's great to spend time listening to customers but now, it's become a bit more scientific, looking at reports analysing figures by department. I've got boring figures all over the place. It's not the same any more – I find it hard and a bit dull at times and I know my dad definitely would.

'We have growing pains, which will probably never stop. We have space problems, a cash flow problem... Then you've got a management problem and an EPOS system problem, a stock problem, or a problem in the Far East office. We closed our Hong Kong office. There are always problems that we are faced with all the way along.

'Of course my dad and me don't agree on everything. Sometimes we do pull each other in opposite directions. If we are at loggerheads, more

often than not we can come to a decision. Sometimes I give way to him and other times he gives way to me. It is very good to have each other because it's almost like having a partner on your shoulder. Even if I want to make a decision now, and Dad has admitted it to me, where he has been thinking, "What would Christopher say?" "What would Christopher do?" I think, "What would Dad do now?" "What would he say if I did this and it was wrong?" It is as if my dad has become my own subconscious.

'The TV documentaries were great publicity but they were not for me; I kept out of the way. There is so much work to be done it would have been a distraction. You should see the time it takes! Nothing is quick with producers. I wouldn't have the patience; I know when I've got everything going off in my head, I just couldn't do it for the TV cameras. That's the first reason. Secondly, I just don't think I want to be on TV; I don't think I want it. It is good for the business but as my dad is happy to go in front of the cameras, I think I'll keep out of the way. I'm not saying he's got loads of time, but he has a little more time than I've got. The buying just sucks up 90 per cent of my time.

'I remember when we first started importing and the stuff we imported then was very different to what we import now. Dad and I went to China together for several years, from when I was fifteen until my early twenties. Then I started going on my own, which was a bit scary, to say the least. The first time

it was, anyway, but it has made me more confident – I was very confident in some ways, but not in others. I used to work on the markets, so engaging with people was never a problem. Yet when I started work properly, when I was sixteen, I never used to like picking up the phone to suppliers – I would find it uncomfortable. Looking back, I can see how much business has helped me to grow in confidence. It helped me enormously to grow up.

'Going back to China, I can remember we bought, and I think this was Dad's idea, a lot of ceramic stuff. Now we don't do anything in ceramic. One reason is that it breaks, and the other is that it doesn't sell. One of the ceramic pieces was called a frog on a swing. It sounds ridiculous but it was a ceramic frog on a swing dangling from a ceramic tree. We only had about twenty-five shops at the time but we used to buy and sell these strange items by the container-full! We couldn't keep the shelves filled quickly enough and in the end we sold thousands of them. Sadly, it was very fashionable; nowadays I don't think you could give them away! Times were different then. People seemed to like their homes full of ornaments in those days, now it's all much more minimalistic and nobody wants pot frogs on swings. At the time anything ceramic sold well – we even sold a lot of ceramic pigs!

'There are loads of bargains at our shops. Standout products include your everyday essentials. Toothpaste is much better value with us and so is

Listerine mouthwash. Crisps and biscuits are all cheaper from our shops. Teabags are a particular bargain – we do 80 teabags for £1 when it's at least two and a half times that price in other shops. There are so many good deals across the board. I am proud that ordinary people can save a lot of money by shopping with us. The good thing is that sometimes you don't think about it as much but when you spend time in the shops, you can see just how much people love the concept. But when you look at what we turn over then what we earn in profits is minuscule. At Poundland they turn over £1.1 billion and earn a profit of £44 million, which is still relatively small for the turnover. If it wasn't for discounters, I don't know how people on a limited budget would cope. They couldn't afford lots of the things we make it possible for them to buy. That's why the discount market has grown; there's a real need for it. What's really good is that people are relaxed in our shops. I've done a lot of market research, which shows this. They just love the concept of everything costing £1. Apparently people on a limited budget often feel terrified of walking into a supermarket. Now I would have thought that I wouldn't walk into a store if I didn't have any money, but if you need something, you have to go in.

'There are so many commodity items that you can't always avoid the inevitable: you have to go in and buy something. All this research we've had done says that people, and not always the ones on

low incomes, are sometimes scared of going to a shop and spending more than they want to spend. So when it's the pound price point, it's very easy to control exactly how much you're spending. If you've only got a fiver to spend, you can buy five items. Simple! Whereas when you go into a supermarket and fill your trolley, everyone knows it always costs more than you thought. Unless you've got a calculator, when the bill comes at the end you're often in for a surprise. I've often been shocked when I'm expecting a total of £80 to find the trolley load adds up to £140! You haven't got that problem when you're shopping in our stores; it's a very simple format. People count the number of items they've got in their baskets and often have the right money ready at the till so there are no nasty surprises.

'Expansion is definitely on our minds: we've got 280 stores and I believe we can certainly get to 500. That is the current ambition. We are spread more thinly in the south. We have more shops down there than we've ever had before. Going back six or seven years, if someone said Scotland, it was like another planet. This was ingrained into me by my dad, who said we would only open a shop within a two-hour drive away; that's why we've got a lot of shops in the northwest and anywhere within that two-hour radius of Yorkshire. We never really expanded south or north into Scotland. We never, ever thought in a million years, even several years ago, that we would have shops in Belfast, or the rest of Northern Ireland,

or Scotland, or shops in London. *Back then it was like thinking of opening a shop on Mars – not a chance! So I think the next stage is getting to 500 stores. Some of them will be further afield. There are some good opportunities in retail parks and then I guess when you get to that 500, you think: "Is that it?" It depends on the circumstances of the business and where we are then. There's always room to grow in England. Poundland are quoting 1,000 stores. We have research showing there's definitely room for hundreds more stores. Then we've got Europe and the question becomes: "Where do you stop?"*

'*I am fortunate in that, like my dad, I have a lot of energy and I enjoy what I do. Also, like Dad, I am going into another business, a pub restaurant outside Wakefield. My dad has had a conversation with me a hundred times about: "Don't make the mistake I made." But if I ask him if he would change anything, the answer is no. You really can't stop yourself.*

'*I never thought I'd do something like this. My girlfriend said I always insisted I'd never have a restaurant in a million years. I think the only reason I said that was because my dad used to say the same thing. He always insisted there were too many problems with restaurants. Nightclubs and bars were fine, but selling drinks is so much easier than selling food. I thought the same for a long time; I thought I would never have a restaurant. I never even thought I would have a pub, to be honest, but then the opportunity came up.*

'I have a different partner in this enterprise. Funnily enough, I have become really good friends with the guy I bought my house from. He's got a business in Leeds and he told me he was looking at this pub and I said: "Do you know, I quite fancy doing something different." It wasn't like anything my dad had done because I wouldn't want to copy him; I didn't go looking for it, the opportunity was there. I'm pretty sad! I don't have any hobbies – I don't play sport, I don't watch sport. I socialise, I go out drinking; I go out eating. I like going to the cinema and relaxing and I like going on holiday. But I don't really have any interests; I don't read books. I just fancied doing something a bit different. I remember I dreaded the conversation with my dad. Even though I'm thirty-two, I was not looking forward to telling him my plans for opening a pub restaurant. I dreaded it!

'I was looking at him a few months ago and I was about to sign for it and I knew I couldn't keep quiet about it, but I really wasn't looking forward to telling him. So I said: "Can I have a word with you?" I took my laptop up and I showed him. I knew he wasn't going to say: "That's great!" I also knew he wasn't going to say: "That's shit, don't do it!" Or "What are you doing that for?" But I knew he would be thinking, "Don't do it." I just knew he wouldn't really approve, but he couldn't say anything because after all the things he's tried, he would be a hypocrite.

'You do something like the pub restaurant to satisfy a certain need and I think my dad understands and appreciates that: it's not about the money. Of course you like the money if it happens, but to me life is about doing the best you can with what you've got, and the pub is the same. The pub is obviously one pub versus all these stores but it is something I can work on and hopefully succeed with. It is near where I live: in Methley, near Wakefield. So far we're in a honeymoon period and everything is going very well, but I know I can't get complacent. My partner has project managed the development himself and obviously we have shared responsibility on the operational side. I've done all the marketing, design and PR. It's called the Boundary House and it's quite a good building with a nice beer garden; we've put some decking outside so on a hot weekend it should do well.

'Dad has been to visit and I think he was pleasantly surprised. There are still improvements to make but I think on the whole he was complimentary. In fact, I got more praise about the pub than what I have done for Poundworld! I think secretly he got a little bit of a buzz from it. He could see the kick I had got from opening something and I think that triggered some of his own memories. It's great to see an idea taking shape.

'For me it has to succeed. Even if Poundworld were booming, it would infuriate me if the pub made a loss. I know I don't need the money, but it's important to me to do things well. My dad's the same. When one of his clubs is not happening, he *thinks it's a reflection on him and so he asks himself: "How can I not make this work? I've convinced myself I'm good in business, why can't I make this bloody nightclub or this bar work?" I understand that frustration and I would share it, if things go wrong with the pub. But for me it's a distraction. The pub stops me worrying about work. It's not constructive to spend a lot of time sitting at home, stewing over things. The pub restaurant is like a hobby but I certainly don't want it to lose money. I like sitting there and watching people; I like to watch the dynamics of people reacting to my new project. It's a learning process and I'm enjoying it.*

'I like fixing problems. I am interested in people too. I say to my girlfriend all the time: "There's nowt so queer as folk." That's what I love. In our shops you meet all kinds of people and I find it fascinating. You see affluent people coming in, determined to get a bargain, and lower incomes coming in as well. Observing people is one of my hobbies. I like to remain as anonymous as possible for as long as I can. The pub customers don't know me from Adam and in a shop opening, people don't know who I am, and I can see their honest reactions. That's invaluable. The best learning is when no one knows who you are. My dad is recognised from the TV programmes so he can't walk around without being noticed, like I can.

'Our family background is remarkable. All the stories of fairgrounds and trapeze artists are amazing,

but to be honest, I don't regret missing it because it was all years before I was born. It's great to hear about where we came from and my dad's always told me all about it. I know I've got Dad's work ethic – I've been trained over the years in how to work hard. I used to think I just got it from him, but he says he got it from his dad and from generations before. There is a tradition of determination and hard work in our family. I do remember as a little boy, trying to get involved in everything my grandma and grandad did, working very, very hard all the time. When my grandad was officially retired, he still used to work doing odd jobs and repairs and emptying slot machines.

'I know I share that desire to work all the time and obviously my dad does too. He says he doesn't want to retire because he would find it boring. My view is: if I'm only thirty-two, if I carry on working as hard as this then my head might blow off when I'm in my fifties! Or is it just about having a couple of smaller businesses so it's not about the scale, more the creativity? Would I be happy in my fifties with a couple of pubs? I don't know the answer to that yet.

'Dad doesn't have a secretary or a PA and has no email address of his own. That does drive me mad sometimes. He says he hasn't got a PA, but I get his emails! I don't get many, to be honest, because I've said: "Look, either get an email address or send them to somebody else, because I haven't got time to print them out!"

'Dad is a remarkable man. To go from a market stall to a huge chain of stores across the country is an amazing journey he has travelled. He took that first leap with a shop and always tells the story of my grandad saying: "What do you want a shop for?" That's why I think he didn't tell me that with the pub. When I started fulltime, when I was sixteen, he had fifteen or sixteen shops and the nightclubs and was obviously successful. How do you start that from having no money to do it with? How do you know where to buy? My dad learned from Grandad, but he had to find out such a lot for himself as he was breaking new ground all the time. When I started, I knew in a way, from his experiences, what sells and what doesn't. I had a head start; Dad didn't have any of that – he had a market stall, but that was different. A lot of his early time was trial and error. Nowadays, you can trial items in store and experience helps you to tell what goods are going to be in demand.

'Sometimes it is not hard to tell. If mobile phones are selling well, then our chargers and adaptors will also sell well. It's not rocket science! From my dad's point of view, he didn't know at the start – he had to learn – and I have been able to benefit from that knowledge. I know dishcloths are a bestselling line – but does anybody else? For me, I know it, but I know it because Dad has done it. He's had to buy and sell lots of dishcloths to find that out. All those years of experience are invaluable.

'We work pretty well together. We do clash

sometimes and we argue sometimes, but it works. All father-and-son relationships must be a little like us if they're working closely together in the family business. Where we are always on the same page is on the shop floor, on the mechanics of customer service, mentality, drive and work ethic. I think nowadays we have more of a business relationship than a father-and-son relationship. We spend so much time at work that we don't really socialise outside that often, possibly because we're sick of seeing each other. I think my dad always had a similar relationship with Grandad. Dad's my biggest motivator and it was the same with him. He never praised me too much, but if I'd been praised when I was sixteen, would I still be here? You always want to please your dad.

'My own journey has been fairly interesting. After the Far East, I went on another buying trip with Dad to New York. I visited a toy show and I can remember they wouldn't let me in at first because I was underage – you had to be eighteen to get in and I was only fifteen. I had to get some fake business cards done. It was an experience. But definitely, when I went to China, it was tough: we were not then where we are now in business. Today, we go business class and stay in decent hotels. Back then it was the cheapest possible airline and hotel.

'Once I cried because I didn't want to go. Deep down, I really did want to go, but it wasn't easy in those days. In the cab on the way to the airport I cried. I hated the idea of being squashed in an awful *airline seat for fourteen hours and then, when we got there, we used to have a coach to China, and no kidding, it would take about six hours! It was full of Chinese people and stopping all the time, you got no rest and you had to get off and then on again. It was horrible! As a kid I really dreaded the coach journey even more than the flight – it was my nightmare, really hot and stuffy.*

'*Then the hotel was called the Dong Fang hotel in Guangzhou. It was filthy and cockroach-infested. Dad and I used to share a room to keep the overheads down. I loved the work going to the trade show but the bit I hated was travelling and the evenings, because in the evenings I was with men. I felt uncomfortable so sometimes I would stay in my hotel room and watch television or a DVD or something and my dad would go out and have a few drinks. Now it's different but it's good that I've seen that more difficult, early side. It went on for three or four years. We used to do it on an absolute shoestring then gradually it began to improve. We still travelled economy but stayed in slightly better hotels. As we were buying more, we could justify our overheads more. Now, it's not a problem and it's quite nice travelling – I quite enjoy having a chill-out on a plane.*

'*The good fortune of my being the right age at the right time is definitely key to everything. Dad always used to drop me off after school and I would sit in his office. When I was sixteen, we used to share an office. Then, when Mark started, he used to sit in there as well. The three of us were in one small room and that was the management.*

'Where the years go, I don't know. Dad said you lose your twenties and he was right. One thing he pushed me to do, which I am really happy about: I was twenty-one and my friends went to America for two weeks. I said: "I can't come, we're too busy." We'd had this booked for six months or longer. The week before we were going, I was out with them all and they were saying all the things they were going to do, and I felt very left out and jealous.

'I was a single lad at the time – I had just split up from my girlfriend – and they were talking about all these different fun things they were going to do and I was unhappy. I think Dad picked up on my mood and asked me what was wrong. I explained that my friends were going away the following week, a big group of lads going to LA, New York, Vegas. It was a big trip before they all settled down, big blowout of twenty-one-year-olds. I should probably have gone, but I had said no, I told him. Dad said: "You're going." And he booked everything for me. He booked it, and paid for it, and said: "There you go, you're going."

'So I went, and that two weeks of my life was probably the best I've ever had; it was great! I was so glad I went, and even to this day, my friends still talk about it. That was the last two-week holiday I had. Dad has been good in that way. Now he knows not to question or interfere too much, but then I was

young enough for him to step in and take over. I needed a nudge.

'The growth of Poundworld is down to a combination of everything. On the buying side, we are stocking the top brands and quality imports. We first used to play at imports and just bring a few bits in, but it has become a major thing. We bring in seventy or eighty containers a week. At Christmas, it's 120 containers a week. It's a massive operation compared to the old days. When I first started doing the ordering of containers, before EPOS and before I really started doing the buying, a man would come and say to my Dad: "Chris, we've got no coat hangers left." One of the first things we used to import was a mixed container of dryers, coat hangers and pegs. All plastic, it had to be packed in a container. They're really bulky so Dad was determined to fill a container up, even if we only had twenty-five or thirty shops at the time. But if we ran low on stock, it took time to get a delivery from China!

'My Uncle Laurie always struggled to get his head round the time involved. He thought, "I'm out of stock, I'll ring up and get a delivery in tomorrow." That happened so many times, I got involved – "Let me see if I can help," I said. I could tell, because I was always out in the shops, merchandising, that we would often run out of stock of good sellers so I said: "Let me try to put a plan in to organise the buying so we don't end up being out of stock of these items."

'I used to handwrite my order on a piece of paper

and then work out on my office calculator how much space it was going to fill on the container and then fax my order to China. I would have this little tray on my desk and funnily enough, Mark Ward still has the same tray on his desk. You can still see my handwriting from when I was sixteen. Faxing a piece of paper was how primitive it was, back then. Mind you, even the fax machine was revolutionary. When I first started, I asked: "Where's the computer?" The answer was: "Where's the what? We just have typewriters." In fact, they had one computer in the building – in the accounts department.

'*But I think it's very good that I came into the business in time to see the huge change. If I'd come in later and not seen all that, I wouldn't be where I am. In a way, the timing was perfect. I was sixteen and Dad had enough stores and was offered that opportunity to go to China – and he asked me to come. That is probably the key point in my life! I don't think many dads would have asked their fifteen-year-old son to come along – they would have been keener to get them to go to university. I went to private school and I wouldn't say it was a waste of money because they taught me discipline. Our family has a tradition of doing things together and Dad called on me when he needed me. Timing wise, I do think: "Was it just meant to be? Were we somehow meant to have this growing business and create all these jobs?"*

'*When you think about it, the responsibility does blow your mind a little. It's brilliant to create something. The big one for me is when Dad says: "You don't know what it's like to have nothing." I say back: "You don't know what it's like to grow up with that risk of losing everything hanging over you." I do worry that if things go wrong, I could become that guy who took over from his dad and lost everything: the risk of losing everything hangs heavily over me.*

'Dad's the same – he still worries about losing everything. We've had this conversation between ourselves; it's like a constant burden, if you like. Of course I enjoy running the business otherwise I wouldn't do it, but you just have that everlasting fear hanging over you. I always feel I can't have a bad week. I just can't say: "You know what, I'm going on holiday for two weeks." I can't do it!

'I had my first week off in five years in February and went to Barbados. I've had weekends away, several long weekends, but it would be impossible for me to take more than a week. I know it shouldn't be like that and maybe as it becomes a little more structured, I will. Yet that week was massive for me, I really enjoyed it. I thought I was going to worry. The trouble was when I was sitting on the beach I had my iPad there. My girlfriend was reading a book and I was twiddling my thumbs so when an email came through, it gave me something to do for a minute.

'I didn't get bombarded, but I wasn't out of touch – it just gave me that reassurance. It doesn't matter about holidays too much at the moment, but hopefully

in time, I'll have a little bit more time off, but when there is so much going off, I just think I want to try and stay on top of it. If I stay on top of my work, then mentally at night or at the weekends, I feel better. So I work hard to feel better, like my dad.

'I think in a way the deal with the American investors will put more pressure on! Dad wants to do it. I'm not saying I don't want to do it, but there's a big part of me that wants to carry on as we are, independently. Dad has always said: "Don't work for anybody, work for yourself! Don't be answerable to anybody else." That's been ingrained in me so when he came up with something like these American investors taking control, it made me think. I know the time is right so I'm going with it, and I'm happy.

'For me it's not about the money. I will be working with very intelligent people who will bring a lot to the table and teach me a lot on the corporate side. Obviously, Dad and me are not corporate. I think if we left and the corporate people took over completely then the business would fail. And they know that – it's that balance. Me and my dad don't call each other entrepreneurs; I don't like that word, but being that minded, and there's a little more corporate in there we need to understand. Things you miss you don't understand because we've never been taught it. We have never been to a school of business, we have just jumped in and run a business, making mistakes and succeeding through trial and error.

'Often we've got things wrong. Sometimes I find

the corporate jargon uncomfortable. I've met a lot of business people I simply don't understand. I'd have to use Google to find out what some of the jargon means. Then I realise what they are talking about is simple! My dad and I are the same in many ways: neither of us has been to university or business school but we both know how to run a business successfully. Our business is extremely simple: we buy things and we sell them. But we do accept that there are things we can learn from our investors and we look forward to working with them.'

Where it all changed, I think, was when my son started, sixteen years ago. He had just left school, but he certainly made an instant impact. By the time he was seventeen or eighteen, he was forcing lots of issues with me. By then I had been at retail a long time and I was getting a bit tired – a lot of late nights with the nightclub business had made me feel very weary.

Louise and my daughters thought I had some sort of an affliction because my eyes were always bloodshot. It showed when I was really tired and they would say: 'Your red rims are back!' It meant I'd been doing too many late nights. I was thinking, 'Where am I going to go with this?' Although I kept my concerns to myself, there was a period when I questioned where I was heading in the future.

The arrival of my son in the business changed all that: the youthful energy and creative ideas he put into the business were terrific and had a hugely uplifting impact on me. I never lost my sense of direction or the ability to work hard, but I needed help, and Christopher provided that. He found a way, using his education and looking at the whole operation and coming up with positive plans. Everything we had, he reconfigured. He took a new look at how we went about our business and set about bringing it up to date brilliantly.

If I've got a failing, it is that I fly by the seat of my pants a little too often. That does allow me to punch above my weight sometimes but as the business grew, it clearly needed someone like Christopher to take a fresh look at the overall picture. He came in and injected a bit of a structure, shook it all up a little and tried to make changes. With his ideas about re-branding and bringing in the EPOS system, he gave us just the shot in the arm we needed.

I'm convinced most highly corporate businesses are all very carefully preplanned, while others, like Poundworld, are driven more by events and opportunities. I've always felt a lot happens by chance; we're in a 'by chance' environment. It is never planned years ahead, but Christopher helped start the process of taking us into the future, bringing it to new levels.

Just before my son started, I made the decision to turn our shops into Pound shops – that was sixteen years ago. Almost as soon as Christopher started, we realised the single price was working better than the multi-price was doing at the time; it all sort of gelled together. There was never a detailed plan – next year we are going to do this and the year after, we're going to do that – it was just by chance. Everything is just a chance. My son had quite an impact on the business. The woman he overheard saying 'I'm not going in there' was crucial. He's had a massive impact all the way through.

You might have noticed that Christopher has never been on the TV series that the BBC recently made about our business, though, *Pound Shop Wars*. At work, he is highly vocal and very aggressive, but he is a contradiction. Publicly, he is extremely quiet and reserved, while at work he can very, very passionate. I think he's a bit like I used to be: an introvert in the big world, but in his own world he has very strong opinions and is highly vocal. Take him to a pub, and if there are twenty people talking, he'll be the quietest of them all. Put him in his business, and he is forceful and articulate. I was the same: it was not exactly that I'd take no nonsense but simply out of frustration I could become aggressive then I'd pick on people because I was frustrated.

The problem is, as anyone who has a son will understand, we both want the same thing but there is sometimes a clash of personalities. As a father-son relationship, it's not always good. Underneath it's all there, but you never get the chance to show it because there's always another problem, today or tomorrow. Right now, we've just had a hairy moment and we have plenty of heated moments. You can't work all day and then socialise together. I'm not saying we never socialise, but not often: a gap appears and I don't think it's good. On reflection, that's the only downside of what we've done so far. But we haven't lost the connection and we're not enemies; we are close but we don't seem to find the chance to talk about other things, it's all about the business. My son will always be my son and we will always treat each other with respect, but in the agitation of running a business together, making a big decision sometimes causes stress between us.

CHAPTER THIRTEEN

REVITALISED

My son Christopher and Mark Ward started work with me at exactly the right time. I had no idea they would be as dedicated and dynamic as they have turned out to be, but I think that I knew I needed the extra help. Just as Louise helped me with the nightclub business when I needed it most, so Christopher and Mark helped with the shops.

I had just passed fifty and I was feeling every year. My brother Laurie had recently had a bit of ill health. It wasn't life threatening, but it meant he wasn't there for me to lean on quite so much. If I'm honest, I was still missing my dad and I was starting to wonder if I wanted to keep on working so relentlessly for much longer. Put simply, I was weary and I was beginning to falter.

By the time Christopher was sixteen, I'd had sixteen years of nightclubs to go with my demanding role running the shops.

By 1999, we had only nine shops but the turnover was £4 million and we were trying to grow. I'd been working night and day because I used to work nights at the nightclubs and my days were spent doing the buying for the shops. But just as I was beginning to think I might have to slow down a little, Christopher and Mark arrived and that changed everything. The enthusiasm of youth can be a heady tonic, especially when it finds a niche where it can make a difference.

Christopher and Mark were exceptional. They really hit the ground running and lifted the business – and me – with their extraordinary enthusiasm. Very quickly, they seemed to pick up on what needed doing. Almost as soon as they arrived, they brought more energy into the business. It revived me massively. All of a sudden the tiredness seemed to evaporate, I could see the progress we were making and once again, I felt full of beans. With renewed vigour, I threw myself into action and the last sixteen years have simply flown by. Now we've got 300 shops so we've come a long way in a relatively short time. We've earned a lot of credibility and with that credibility, our banking and borrowing gets easier but over the years we've had difficult times with the banks because when you are expanding at a big rate of knots, they don't always find it easy to keep up with you and your needs.

In fact, we've had several banks and there is a whole story with banking. We started with NatWest and Mr Shackleton – he was great to work with. When I wanted to do the nightclubs, we had a bit of a dip but we got round it somehow. We were settled in with NatWest for a while but as soon as you get a bit too big, I find, you start to worry a bank and if their mentality can't run with yours, then you've got to make the move.

One of the best banking periods we had was with the Bank of Scotland. In recent years, we've had a relationship with several different banks but before that we had a ten year association with the Bank of Scotland, which was great. Unfortunately, when the great banking crisis arrived, the Bank of Scotland was one of the casualties. We found ourselves with a different bank and about five years ago, they came into our headquarters at Normanton and said: 'Right, we're now your bankers.' Our business had been handed over to them without us having any say in the matter. It was not a happy experience. They came in and said: 'This is what we're going to do.' In one meeting they announced they were going to inflict £10,000-a-week in extra overheads onto us from a raised percentage of the borrowed money and an increase in the cost of our cash banking charges. They said: 'You need us.' We did need our banking facility because in this business now we need trade insurers to be onside with us. We need suppliers to be comfortable with our banking set-up so they are prepared to give us stock on terms. At the end of that first meeting, I told them we needed time and so they gave us a week to think about it.

I went back to Allied Irish Bank, which is the bank Annis Abrahams had introduced me to when he sold me his Mecca club, which I renamed Dollars. They have been my personal bankers ever since. I wanted advice. I asked for a meeting with them. I wanted to know more about how the banking world works. AIB are not a big, upfront bank, but they are very personal. In the old days they would ask you in for a cup of tea while they counted the cash – it was always very friendly. By then I'd been with them twenty-seven years, and so I went and told them about my problem with our new bankers. 'Look, these are the tactics they're using on me. Can you advise me how to push them back?' I said. The manager told me: 'By the sound of it, and from what I know about the bank, there might be a problem. Our advice to you is to patronise them and find another bank.'

The following week, we had another meeting. Four of them came in, all suited and booted and very corporate. As I watched their cold, expressionless faces, I fully intended to follow the advice I'd been given and patronise them. Round here, we are very casual and they sat at the boardroom table and said they hoped we had given what they had said some thought because we had got to move on.

In that week we had approached several banks. We knew we had got another bank more or less onside, as they had agreed that if we needed funding, they would step in. As I looked at the executives staring arrogantly back at me, I said: 'Look, I'm going to be totally 100 per cent honest because that is the only way I can be. I've been advised to patronise you, but unfortunately, I haven't got a patronising bone in my body. So what I'm saying is, don't mess me about and try and bankrupt this company on the back of my words. I'll make sure we've got everything in motion if you just back me up for three to four weeks. I'll re-do the banking facilities and make sure you get your money back.'

I can't recall exactly how much we owed them at that point. It might have been £6 or £7 million. Anyhow, it was a lot of money. They left, and I noted everything we had borrowed from them was on overdraft. I told the finance director to get the overdraft onto the maximum because it's a known fact that if a bank is ever going to pull the plug, they love to get in credit and cut your overdraft off. 'They can't cut it off, if it's on maximum,' I said. For four weeks we kept the overdraft at its maximum so they had no money to take. As the money came in, we kept it flying out, but the future of the business hung in the balance. Ian, who was our finance director at the time, got in touch with the local branch of our latest banking hope. Of course they came in, all singing, all dancing, because they get big bonuses on the back of new business.

They offered us a minimum deal for our finances. Even though it was classified as an overdraft, it was broken down into two parts: one like a normal overdraft that you could understand, and the other was an import loan facility. They offered to give us the same deal as we had had before, which was OK, but the problem was by the time we'd been coming out of the Bank of Scotland and getting involved with all this negotiating, even though it was only a short time, we had opened twenty more shops. Those shops were straining the facility because obviously you've got to buy stock for another twenty stores so the facility we had was strained anyway. But we were happy to get away from our existing bankers, who we thought were really bad bankers – extremely aggressive and wanting to milk us for all they could get.

The new people appeared to be very charming and apparently much more amenable. That was fine, but we'd been holding back on payments with suppliers and things to try and make the transition work.

By this time we were creeping towards August and September. In retail, when you're importing stock and you're paying for all of it before you actually get it, there are times when your finances become strained, particularly when you are trying to expand. All the containers were building up in the docks, and our debts were building as well. As I've said, we were with the Bank of Scotland for ten years. Throughout that time, they were well aware that from January through to July the facility we had was good and perfectly adequate, but from August into September, October and November, we just needed what we used to call a 'temporary extra top-up' that helped to pay for the containers that were coming in. With a bank that understood our philosophy and how we were operating, it was never a problem: we would just take extra money some time in August and pay them back in the first week of January. That was how we had always done it.

How it works is that we have a facility that works for eight or nine months of the year. Then, when we're getting our Christmas stock in from the Far East, obviously we have to get the stock in plenty of time before we make the sale. For that first eight or nine months we are basically turning round stock constantly. Then, when the spike for Christmas comes, we are paying for stock we are not going to be selling for a month, two months or even three months. Our cash flow goes out of kilter. Therefore, what we do is increase our overdraft by 50 per cent but when the stock turns into cash, we can quickly reduce that. With the Bank of Scotland, we used to have a facility whereby we would have our overdraft increased by a third, get over Christmas, and then pay it back once we had turned the stock over. But that's what spooked our new bankers.

We tried to explain all that to the new bankers and they said: 'Yes, don't worry, just hit us when you're ready and we'll get over it.' Well, they didn't get over it because we opened fifty shops in twelve months and we wanted to double our overdraft! I wish there had been a facility for fifty extra shops; this spike in money for a small period was twice as much as it had ever been because we had opened so many stores. So when the local manager came in and said there was an extra £2 million available, we had to ask for £8 million or possibly £10 million. If we had had that extra facility, we wouldn't have had a problem but that was beyond their remit as a local branch, so they said: 'We can't authorise that, we've got to go to the main office. So people from London came here to see us in Normanton. It was another group of unsmiling, expressionless people in suits. The words they actually used were: 'We think you've lost control of this business.' That was only three years ago. 'What makes you think that?' I said. They replied with a load of pompous waffle and suggested we had misinterpreted our position.

'Well,' I told them, 'if we have misinterpreted our position, we have just misinterpreted how many opportunities there are to open new shops. Bear in mind that although we rent all the shops, we pay for all the fittings, the EPOS equipment, the tills, etc. We pay for everything as we go. So, since we've been with you we have probably opened twenty or thirty shops of that fifty. We spent on average £120,000 a shop on fittings.' They had also said to me: 'We can't go on funding your business.' So I said: 'If we're paying for the shops and you're just funding the stock, I think we're working to leave all the money in the pot to be able to afford all these things. I think the suppliers are funding it, not you. You're just lending the money for the stock.' I was trying to tell them that our overdraft was exactly the same as it had been when we started with them and we had opened twenty or thirty shops and invested £120,000 in each and every shop without increasing that overdraft. They were trying to tell me they were funding the business. I asked how that could be when we had put that money in to increase the size of the business without any help from them.

We had nearly doubled the size of the business on the current facility we had from the bank, and they came in at that point and said: 'We can't go on funding your expansion.' I said to them: 'How are you funding the expansion? We haven't increased that facility whatsoever and we have doubled the size of the business without asking for any more money. How come you think you're funding it?' We were funding it out of cashflow and profit. How could we be using their money if we were still on the same overdraft facility?

But they had major issues and they said before they could lend us the money for this spike, we should bear in mind that all the containers were on the water. We explained that while we might have paid deposits on some of those containers, we would have to pay in full when they arrived in the docks because you get your clearing documents then; it's very controlled. At this point the head man wanted to do what he called 'a scope of works' to make sure we hadn't lost control of the business. Somebody else piped up, asking if the spike in money we needed was so high, why were our figures so good? This is from a bank! They worked out a logical suggestion that if we cancelled some containers and maintained the takings, we wouldn't have a problem. I tried to be patient and said: 'Hasn't it dawned on you? The stock in the containers is what generates the takings!'

They were breathtakingly unhelpful. I think what happened at that time in banking was that people who weren't fit for a job were finding their way into one because they were laying so many people off. The banking world was in such a mess you got some right idiots in jobs. With their crombies and their dark suits, they might have looked the part, but in business terms I wouldn't have trusted any of them to run a bath!

I think they were close to pulling the plug on us. They brought in an advisor and I could see in his eyes that he was considering telling the bank to withdraw all of our credit facility. To me he was the equivalent of a liquidator, and they are born robbers. He was looking on and thinking, 'There is all this stock and they only have that small overdraft. The bank who have employed me are already thinking this business is out of control.' In fact, he would have known we weren't out of control but had he advised the bank accordingly, they could have pulled the plug. Fortunately, that didn't quite happen but it was a close thing and that was only three years ago.

I believe there are some very successful businesses that have gone bust simply because they got on the wrong side of the banks. It was obvious to us when we were holding all the stock we had and the overdraft at the time was under control. This was what I tried to point out when they were trying to tell me I'd lost control. It didn't make sense and that's why I got in some heavy-hitters from our accountants, KPMG. I had to bring them in so that when this adviser and the bankers returned, I had someone speaking up for us. Before then, more than once I had woken up in the middle of the night, knowing they could pull the plug on our business. So I didn't tell the bankers that KPMG were coming and the adviser got the shock of his life when he saw them, a week later. It was very different to the first meeting. The adviser's attitude was totally different when he realised I had professionals speaking up for me. He might have thought he had a market man on the run – that's what I identified with him, that he was ready to pull the plug on our business. KPMG came in and stabilised the whole situation so the bank were listening to my advisers, as well as their own. It was the adviser to the bank who was causing the trouble rather than the bank but it was still a frightening time.

Anyway, they did a 'scope of work', which cost us £230,000. We had to pay our legal and accounting teams, as well as theirs. Eventually, they gave us the extra money to get over the spike. They said they wanted it back in the first week of January, with which we complied. In the second week in January the guy who had instigated the 'scope of works' said: 'We think we understand your business now.' Great! It had cost me £230,000 to educate him.

There was no choice, we had to do it, but that experience led me to the conclusion that the latest bank was no better than the previous one. I couldn't understand why we couldn't have a relationship like the one we'd enjoyed with the Bank of Scotland: we had never cost them a penny and they had plenty of fees out of us. We had done everything they asked of us; we never bust any covenants or agreements. Everything was done perfectly within our agreement because they had the flexibility: we always told them in plenty of time what we were doing and they always backed us up.

We opened communications with two other banks: Barclays and Santander. Both seemed very amenable. We explained the problems we'd had with our previous bankers. Barclays were very strong on saying: 'Oh, they're not giving you a chance to run the business! We understand retail, they clearly don't.'

All of a sudden we were in talks with two banks with quite different attitudes, it seemed. Although Santander was very supportive, Barclays were the first to make us an offer. Santander went into more detail, saying: 'Look, let us go away and consider further. We think you're not asking for enough money. We think you need more funding.' We were asking for what we thought we could achieve rather than what we really needed but there was no point in asking for money if we thought they would say no. Keeping it low but more than we'd had before would balance it up, I thought.

Santander wanted to treat it one way, while Barclays wanted to treat it the other. We asked for an extra facility, both for the overdraft and the other facility so they had a simpler task. Barclays came back and said: 'Right, we'll do the deal with you. We'll take you out of your current bank.' It worked great! Barclays were very good so we had to go with them. Three months later, Santander came back and said: 'This is the facility we feel you really need.' It was roughly double our existing facility.

Santander were quite insistent: 'This is what you really need,' they kept saying. 'We've looked at your business and while we are the biggest bank in Europe, we want a multi-banking operation in England so we can get a presence and we see you as an ideal client.' Back to being in the right place at the right time! This was just three months after we had signed up with Barclays, but Santander said they would take another three to six months to go through all the channels. The Spanish bank's executive came back eight or nine months after we had signed with Barclays, saying: 'Right, we're ready to go.' But before he started on the journey to get us this big facility, the relationship manager, Paul Watkin, had said to me: 'You're not going to let Barclays match my offer. Whatever I come back to you with, if you think it's good enough, you've got to shake my hand. No written agreements, just shake my hand.' He could tell what type of person I am and he repeated: 'Don't let Barclays match my offer. They are not willing to give you this much money now, but they might be prepared to if they realise we are prepared to make this offer. Shake my hand to tell me I am not going to spend the next three or four or five months getting you this big facility only to find you are going to let them match it.'

'I promise you I won't do that,' I told him.

It went all right and he came in six or seven months after we had signed with Barclays and said: 'There's all the agreements ready to sign.'

'How the hell do I tell Barclays now that I don't want them any more?' I wondered.

In fact, Barclays had been superb. Mark Ward and I went to Barclays to meet the management team who had been supporting us for six or seven months – I think they thought we were going in to ask for more money. So I had to tell them we needed to cease our relationship because we'd got this new deal with Santander. Barclays said: 'Do you want us to take a look at it because we might be able to make an offer in about six months?' But I told them: 'To be honest, we can't wait six months, I've given the guy my word.'

I also promised that if anyone from Barclays round the

table might be criticised by their management, I would speak up for them. If anyone so much as suggested mismanagement had caused them to lose an account so quickly, if they gave me twenty-four hours notice then I would come in and meet anyone they might want me to meet and tell them the Barclays team I had dealt with had been superb. It was just that circumstances had created this opportunity. I would have been more than happy to go in and speak up for them because they hadn't done anything wrong, it was simply that Santander had made us a much bigger offer.

It is two years now since we signed with Santander and they have been fantastic! Basically, instead of seeing us as some sort of downmarket outfit, they see us as a high-profile success story. We achieved the middle ground with Barclays and they helped stabilise the business for eight or nine months, but Santander have more faith in us.

The number of Poundworld shops has increased rapidly, particularly in recent years. In 2005, we had 43 shops. That figure rose to 69 in 2009, then 111 in 2011 and 275 in 2014. Of course it all takes funding so when Santander came in and doubled our facility, not only did they get us to where we needed to be, they also gave us enough money to move forward and continue the expansion. Equally, what also helps with expansion is your credit limits with your suppliers. Trade insurers monitor how much credit you've got. Because suppliers insure their debt with credit insurers, when you've got a minimum facility, credit insurers won't give your suppliers enough to fund what you need. Once your facility is bigger, it's the other way round and then with limits, you can have a lot more. This business is all about cash flow: a bigger, more understanding bank indirectly gives you a stronger relationship with your suppliers.

In the last twelve months we have doubled the value of our business because the shackles we were working under have all been loosened, thanks to the support of Santander. I just can't say how good they have been. We had a fantastic relationship with the Bank of Scotland but I would say Santander are even better, yet we had to go through three or four years of torture. Somehow we managed to keep opening the shops, but only because we were concentrating on the banking. Had they pulled the banking at any one time, and I'm convinced the previous bankers were planning to pull the plug on us, we would have been sunk.

I believe there is always a reason why businesses such as Peacocks went down in 2012. Usually, behind a big store or a chain of stores collapsing is a bank anxious to get their money out. I could see the lack of support in the eyes of the previous bankers and their advisers. In my opinion, they were thinking, 'Wait a minute, we might as well take these out. If we foreclose on them, we can sell the stock and get more than our money back.' Then they always instruct a liquidator, or 'legalised robber' as I like to call them, who can come in and make sure the first people they pay out are themselves. Suppliers are irrelevant. And I've dealt with them on the other side: I've taken shops from the liquidator and I know what they're like. As I've said, as far as I'm concerned, they are legalised robbers. I'd say it to their faces, and I have done!

Behind the scenes there was a lot of turmoil going on and all the while I was trying to keep my staff away from all of it: you've got to look confident and happy to make them feel good about the business. These days we have in excess of 6,000 people working for us. That's an awful lot of people and through it all we've had to pay our staff on time, while the bank was saying: 'We're not sure if we're going to pull the money. Are you going to pay us or not?' I found myself feeling very stressed here in the office and then I would have to walk out with a smile on my face and say: 'Morning, everything all right?' all the while looking as if I was on top of the world. You've got to keep everybody calm because sometimes they do get a sniff of something being not quite right. Even in the warehouse they'll know if supplies are booked in and they won't deliver because you haven't paid for last month's stock because the bank won't give you enough money.

But what's happened is remarkable because we've doubled the value of the business in a short time in spite of all these difficulties with the banks. The potential was all there, busting to get out. So what was the key to open the door and let it all come out and deliver the potential? Quite simply, the funding: the funding is the fundamental part of any business. Market days are simpler because your van empties and fills up, then what money is left is yours. That's a very easy operation to understand. When you have good honest bank managers like Mr Shackleton on your side, it is all very simple because you know and trust the person who is lending you the money and in return, he knows and trusts you too. He talks to you in language you will understand and tells you what you need, and that's great!

Then, when you get into what I call this 'corporate shit', life is quite different because trust is one of the first things to go out the window. In a business like ours you have to deal with one of the top four accountants and none of them will upset the other. Whether they are as 100 per cent honest as they portray themselves is up for questioning, though. When I was working on the market and dealing with Mr Shackleton, our relationship was 100 per cent honest: I told him what I really needed and he tried to do it for me.

Once you move into the world of corporate banking, there is more going on. They are not looking at things from your perspective; every individual seems to be looking after himself. One mistake and he knows he could be out of a job. Following the banking crisis, no one had any money to invest. Individuals were running scared. There were no Mr Shackletons anymore. A bank manager for around thirty or forty years, he understood his customers' needs, but banking is no longer like that.

Fortunately, having gone through all that we have finally found a home where the business is allowed to thrive and that is fantastic. As I have already said, Santander have been great! When they ring up, they talk to us in a way that suggests they know we know what we're doing. They make suggestions too. For example, back to the original import question of exchange rate. We were always gambling when we had a container to pay for at the current rate. If the pound was strong against the dollar, our items would be coming in more cheaply but if the pound was in a bad way, as it was about ten years ago, we bought thinking we were buying stock at one price and then by the time the stock was coming in, we were paying much more. It made a massive difference and destroyed the whole twelve months' profits because it came at Christmas when more stock was coming in than at any other time of year.

Over the years we have managed to develop a tactic of booking dollars in front: you agree to pay for them at an agreed rate so hopefully, you can anticipate the currency fluctuations. Say it's 1.60 to the £ and it later goes up to 1.80, then tough shit! You've got it at 1.60. But we've found it's worth taking the risk. If you book it, you've got to take it. So you've got to book what you think you're going to need, if in fact, they'll let you book that far ahead. So that's another development, booking so many dollars until you get bigger.

Santander came in and said: 'We've looked at your problem here: you need to know what your stock is coming in at.' This was when the dollar was extremely strong, just recently up to about 1.70 to the £. They said: 'How many dollars are you going to need for two years?' Now, that really made us think: we considered the question and then we gave them an astronomical figure. They let us book the dollars for two years. So every month now that we are paying for stock, we are getting the benefit of buying at somewhere between 1.65 and 1.70, whereas if we were paying spot, then currently, we would be getting maybe 1.54. So we have doubled the profit of the business, the net profit, because of all the measures that Santander have put in place for us.

Santander have been so supportive of us and the change in attitude moving from our previous bankers to them has been extraordinary. We are working with a friend and not a foe, it seems. And it makes a massive difference. We have only been with Santander for about two years but they want us to continue the expansion. They always ask about the next development and they have invited me to so many functions. In fact, they have even asked me to speak at a few functions for them! They seem to like my 'market man' background and see it as a strength: 'Come and tell our people what you are doing,' they say. Although I still have my 'market man' mentality, I realise now that I find myself in another world.

Of course the bank has no real concept of what I have done but then again not many people have. They have never had to sell the contents of a van every week in order to pay the mortgage and feed the family. If someone asks me how I manage to run a large business, well, it's easy: remember the market. Now that's hard work because you're buying it, you're selling it, you're getting rained on; you're getting snowed on, too. Cash is very limited. What you've got is what you've got in your pocket; you've got nothing else. You can't store it anywhere, you can't buy it cheap enough; you've got to live on your wits. There's no one to teach you what to buy. There's no product range, you just have to buy what you see. You're walking round wholesalers in their showroom, thinking, 'I wonder if I can sell that.' That's the hard part. Poundworld has its ups and down, but I know which one I prefer!

There are plenty of people who are full of big ideas about what they want to do in business, but they would never torture themselves for fifteen years working on markets to get there. It's a hard life at the bottom, where your living is under threat the whole time. You know you could have had a bigger house or a bigger car, or taken more holidays. They would never deprive themselves of that simply to wait and to build up a business.

The lowest point of the discussions with the bankers was terrifying because I was well aware that they could pull the rug from underneath me if they chose to do so. This time there was no kindly Mr Shackleton thinking, 'Is he a good lad?' I can remember him saying: 'You've got an honest pair of eyes.' That was the human side of banking but it's all gone out the window now.

Of course the bankers knew what the agenda was when they took over from the Bank of Scotland. They knew what we were paying for the cash banking, what we were paying to have the facility in the first place, the arrangement fees and all that. So they looked at it and decided, 'Right, he's only paying so much so we're going to do this and that.' And they worked out twelve months of expenses and said: 'Right, this is your deal.' I worked it out: that deal would have cost us an extra £10,000 a week! They put costs on us, banking costs, and had I gone with them at that time, it would have cost me £500,000 a year extra! That's why I told them I needed some time to think about it. And it was a big enough fee to put us out of business at that time.

The meeting with the bankers was attended by Mark Ward, our financial director at the time, and myself – I try to keep Christopher free from this sort of meeting because he always has too much work to do and he can only do so much. I know he realises the banks have to be managed and I try to do that while he manages all the suppliers. If our facilities get tight, he has to handle the suppliers and keep the payments in the right order. He is aware of the stress and so he manages the suppliers while I manage the money to try and make the situation better.

When it comes to money being very, very tight, there is a plus because you are restricted in what you can buy. When you have more money, you are not so restricted. The challenge now is, I've got three big warehouses and they're all full! So we've gone from having no money to having more money for stock. Money gives you more opportunities. In retail, and in wholesale now as well, it's all about what stock you've got – that's what creates the takings. Your warehouse might be full, but then someone says 'That'll fly out' and of course you can't resist it!

CHAPTER FOURTEEN

AND FINALLY...

There was no champagne celebration when the deal was finally signed for TPG to buy 75 per cent of our business for £150 million on 15 May 2015. It was more business as usual. The family still owns the other 25 per cent and as I said earlier, in the introduction to this book, my son Christopher and I will be staying in place to do the same jobs. The takeover will help to accelerate our expansion over the next few years and these are exciting times at Poundworld. My brother Laurie has decided to retire and although I'll miss him, I quite understand this decision. As I've said earlier, he's had some ill health and now he wants to relax and enjoy his travelling.

But I'm definitely carrying on. For me, the money won't change anything. Some people might think it's daft, but in this business I have always had a philosophy where I treat a penny, £1, £100, £1,000, £100,000 or £1,000,000 or whatever sum of money, with the same respect. They're all important but whatever the amount, they get the same treatment from me and from all of us. Maybe that's how daft we are as a family, but our feet will be staying firmly on the ground.

When Christopher earned his very first cash as a young boy, selling stuff with his grandma, she banked it for him in the same branch of NatWest in Wakefield where I borrowed my first money from Mr Shackleton. Ever since then, with all my son's ventures my mum has put the money into that same branch. After we did the deal with TPG, she walked in with a very large cheque and put it into the very same bank account. If only Mr Shackleton had been there to see some of the results of what he had helped to start all those years ago!

Christopher and I are still 100 per cent involved in running the business but I don't think we've fully come to terms yet with what's happened. So, do I feel different? Yes, I do. Do I feel more secure because I've put money in the bank? Yes, I do. Have my heart and my head been in conflict? Yes, and they still are, really. Do I run the business in same way? Well, they've introduced several people. I'm the chief executive officer and they've introduced an executive chairman, a nice guy called Steve Johnson, who has done lots of other big retail jobs. As it happens, he's all right, but I've never had a boss in my life since my dad gave me my head all those years ago. So these are interesting times. Everybody's trying to give help and understanding and I hope we can all work together well.

One of the biggest shocks I've had, after doing this job for a lot of years, is that some of my own staff seem to have had their heads turned. They seem to think that because we as a family are no longer majority shareholders and we've sold out for quite a lot of money, maybe I'm not carrying the same responsibilities or the same authority as before. For me it has been a massive disappointment, it really has. Naturally, I'm challenging it – don't get me wrong, I'm not going to be pushed over that easily. I'm just surprised and disappointed that they have been a bit disrespectful. Not all of them, just a few. I think they feel, 'Who is making the decisions?'

So I had a word with Steve Johnson and I said: 'Look, I think we need to clear this up. It is not us and them; we should all be working together for the same goal. We've got people wondering whether they are taking orders from you or from us. We're not sending the same message, all we're doing is confusing people.' I've asked him to make clear who is going to be doing what in this position. I'm happy to pass over a lot of responsibilities because I've done it for too long. He has actually told me in those six weeks he has found that he leaves here with his head buzzing at the end of the day. Of course he's only just started from the very top of the situation here, working his way down, for just six weeks. Every day for my last forty years I have been working from the shop floor upwards. He has admitted to me that it's already a challenge.

His first words to me after he had been here for just two weeks were: 'You're like Action Man, you're jumping about all over the place!' So I tried to explain that we started this business from nothing and I haven't had time to write these thick reports on just about everything that his sort of management demands. I understand the need for the changes and why they have bought the business; I understand they need these reports. I understand, but that was never in my remit simply because I didn't have the time to get all these people to do all these jobs and write all these reports. I couldn't afford them anyway. So Action Man was the only option I'd got, jumping about and giving quick answers. In two weeks he had identified that and said: 'Can you slow down a bit because I've got to share some of these questions and answers with you?' And I've tried to slow down; I've tried to understand what they're doing. I come into meetings – we now have board meetings and more new executives. We've got quite a cross section of people now dealing with the business and it's very, very different to how we started.

To be frank, I have had one other clash with Steve. He did something which made me very angry. He asked my son Christopher: 'Why is your dad still here, because he's got his money?' Christopher told him that was something he should ask me himself. I didn't mind him asking the question, but as he was leaving the office, he said to Christopher: 'I'd prefer it if your dad didn't know we'd had this conversation.'

It preyed on Christopher's mind for a while but eventually he told me and I was fuming when I heard he'd asked him to keep something from me. Steve had just come back from his holidays and we talked about a few differences we have. The next day, I confronted him and I swore quite colourfully at him and told him what I thought about his conversation with my son. He said it had been taken out of context but I don't really understand that. As far as I'm concerned, he was bang out of order, telling my son to keep something from me. I then said that I wanted to come back from my swearing at him back to a business level of dealing with each other. And I added: 'But don't ever go behind my back ever again.' Since then things seem to be getting better.

I'm trying to embrace it all and I want everybody to be happy. Most of all, I want to be respectful of the people who have invested all this money because they have given me security, which really I have never had in my whole life before. My overdraft was always bigger than my bank account, and when you're in that situation every day, there is not much room for error. Besides, Steve has previously been chairman of Woolworths, he knows retail and he is one of a number of high-calibre people who have been brought in.

It's an education and I'm sure my son will adapt to it a lot better than I will. Maybe I'm a bit long in the tooth to not exactly take orders, but certainly to receive instruction. We'll see... I have never taken instruction in my life before and I'm certainly finding it 'unusual', but I'm not saying I'm finding it difficult.

I'm happy to say the fear of being skint has gone. I no longer wake up in sweats at night and I think it's going to disappear 100 per cent once I get the chance to think about it. I've discussed it with Christopher and all we're talking about all the time is the business, and going forward. We've never gone out and had a drink together, saying: 'Let's celebrate because now we are secure in life.' For us, the money is so secondary to the situation.

So, has the fear gone? Well, as I write this we're only six weeks into it and I'm too busy going to these meetings and thinking about what will be said. I haven't had a chance to deal with the big changes yet; it's just something I want to get over. And I should be able to relax a little. After all, I've got some money in the bank! At the moment it doesn't feel like that, it just feels like everything's different at work. I've not really thought about the money in the bank and my son says he feels exactly the same way.

Although the pressures have changed, the future of the business is still the main concern for Christopher and me. One of the real positives to come out of the deal is that the rate of expansion will speed up. If we hadn't done this deal, it was still our intention to expand. TPG are looking to open 200 shops in three years. We would probably have opened fifty shops a year anyway so we would have opened somewhere between 130 and 150 – they just want us to up the pace a little. Already we were planning to build a 500,000 square foot warehouse near our existing base at Normanton. We were going to do that irrespective of whether the takeover went through. Although we would have been doing it on a shoestring, we had still managed to negotiate ourselves into a position where someone was prepared to spend about £25 million on the new warehouse. We were not paying that; we were going to rent it. We'd done a good job of convincing them that we could pay the rent when we'd built it. The new people have come in and taken an overview, spent six weeks looking at it to see that we have made the right decision, and fortunately they agree. We had to be sure before we entered into negotiations whereas they just said: 'It's great!' It's good having a crystal ball afterwards. What they actually said was: 'Yes, you made the right decision, but you should have been building it six months earlier because you're going to need all that warehouse space before Christmas.' Well, it won't be the first Christmas when we've been short of warehouse space.

Defining my own role has never been easy. My son once came

to me and said: 'What do you actually do?' How I answered that question was to say: 'Well, I've done the buying, I've done the stacking of the warehouse, I've done the loading of the vans, I've done delivery... I've done all the jobs, I've done the wages; I've even done my own VAT returns. So I have done everything in this business.' Now it has grown of course my role is different. I answered Christopher as honestly as I could: 'I'll tell you exactly what I do: I patrol the perimeter. Every time somebody tries to jump the fence and penetrate any of our defences, I've got to get them, that's my job.' But now I'm sharing it, because that's Steve Johnson's job as well.

TPG use a built-in team from what they call the 'mothership'. A worldwide company, they allegedly rarely buy into a business as small as ours. They have an office in London and many more offices worldwide; they are very active too. So far, we have had two board meetings. They have got three people on site at the moment. One is Steve Johnson, who will be staying, another is the supply chain guy, Steve Gardener, who is only here for six months and he is the one who has quantified we have made the right decision over the warehouse. Then there is a statistics guy, who is working very closely with our financial director, Mark Healy. So there are the three of them onsite, and then we have a board meeting and more people come up from London to keep a check on the figures and progress.

So far I feel very committed, but I am still very easily upset... *very* easily! As long as I get respect, everything will be fine. We still own 25 per cent of the business so we have a big chunk of an investment here. A few weeks after the deal had gone through, Mark Healy asked me how I felt and I said one half of me wished I'd never done it, while the other half is very pleased with the deal. My head tells me I have secured the future of the business and done the right thing, but my heart is perhaps still making its mind up. My relationship with my business is very personal: I still get up at the same time and I come to work at the same time. In myself, I haven't changed, but it has taken fifty years to put the business together so it's going to take quite a while to adjust to the change and get back out of it. At the moment I am still reacting the same way.

It's not easy to explain how I feel after selling the majority share of Poundworld but a recent article in *The Sunday Times* by an extremely wise businessman and writer called Luke Johnson captured my emotions perfectly. He said when a founder sells his business it can have a profound impact, almost like a bereavement. This might sound a little over the top, but for me it's true.

Johnson wrote: 'For a founder, running a business is not the same as any other job. It is likely to be an all-consuming passion, a whirlwind, an obsession, and a high stakes gamble. It is more than just their work and their fortune – it is their identity and their life's purpose. So when they sell, it can be devastating – but also sometimes a great release, after the years of stress and responsibility. Yet once entrepreneurs have sold out, what do they do? For some, it will have been the first time they have really made money. So they go ahead and buy the presents they promised themselves as a reward for all the toil – a bigger house, a ski chalet, a boat. They travel the world. One-shot founders feel no need to prove themselves a second time; they do not long for the status or challenges. But many get bored quickly, missing the sense of adventure and meaning that building a company gave them. And some suffer chronic seller's remorse, describing the emotion after their exit as almost like mourning.'

He certainly knows what he's talking about. At the moment I am still fully involved with Poundworld but I'm still coming to terms with the sale. When the news broke that the deal had gone through, I was in Bradford with the BBC people. They wanted to finish off one of the programmes from *Pound Shop Wars*, the eight-part series on Poundworld which was screened in the summer and autumn of 2015. I was actually outside our second-ever shop. The BBC wanted to film there and ask me my thoughts about that shop. So we did that and my mum was with me, then I got a call from Mark Ward, one of our directors. He rang to say: 'Right, the deal's done!'

I said: 'Right, OK, thanks.' Then I said to my mother: 'That was Mark on the phone, we've done that deal.' Mum chirped up: 'Well, will I keep my job?' I said: 'They'll probably say to me, "Will you get rid of your bloody mother?"' Quick as a flash as usual, she came back: 'Will I get paid redundancy?' 'Well, you've only done sixty-three years' service so you'll probably get about £4 million quid. I'd settle for redundancy, if I were you,' I told her. 'I'll have it!' she said.